A NATURALIST'S GUIDE TO THE

REPTILES
OF
THE PHILIPPINES

T0312790

Emerson Y. Sy

JOHN BEAUFOY PUBLISHING

Reprinted in 2024

First published in the United Kingdom in 2023 by John Beaufoy Publishing Ltd
11 Blenheim Court, 316 Woodstock Road, Oxford OX2 7NS, England
www.johnbeaufoy.com

Photo captions and credits
Front cover *main image* McGregor's Pitviper © Charls Lee S. Ibañes; *bottom row, left to right* Green Sea Turtle © Rhett Arthur Diana, Forest Lizard © Don Geoff Tabaranza, Northern Luzon Forest Monitor Lizard © Emerson Y. Sy.
Back cover Philippine Forest Turtle © Yñigo del Prado
Title page King Cobra © Erickson Tabayag
Contents page Günther's Flying Lizard © Jay Paul E. Mantuon

Photo Credits
Main descriptions are denoted by a page number followed by t (top), b (bottom), m (middle), l (left), r (right).
AA Yaptinchay 15, **Aaron Hilomen** 152t, **Adrian Constantino** 23b, **Alexander Dalabajan** 57t, 94, **Alvin De Guzman** 158tr, **Andrie Bon Flores** 150, **Angel Gabriel Pineda** 110b, 158t, 161mr, **Anre Kuizon** 28, **Athena Heart Lobos** 158bl, **Brian T. Sabanal** 78, 155, 161t, **Charls Lee S. Ibañes** 159, **Chiang Chih Wei** 48t, **Christian E. Supsup** 31b, 39, 64t, 70, 87, 99, 129, 143, **Cyrus Dela Cruz** 32t, 107, 133, 134t, **Dante A. Oporto** 162b, **Don Geoff Tabaranza** 31m, 77b, 83, **Elsa May Delima-Baron** 97, **Emerson Y. Sy** 10, 11, 16, 19t, 20b, 21tb, 23t, 24tb, 31tl, 32b, 34, 36, 38tb, 40, 42tb, 43t, 44, 45, 46, 47tb, 49, 54t, 55t, 56t, 57b, 59t, 60b, 67, 71, 74, 76, 81, 88bl, 90, 96, 101, 102bl, 110t, 119b, 122, 125b, 128, 131tb, 134m, 136b, 137tb, 152b, 154tlr, 157r, **Eric Claire Selpa** 91, 158tl, **Erickson Tabayag** 13b, 22, 27, 65t, 157l, **Erl Pfian Maglangit** 54b, **Flavio A. Nava** 148b, **Gerrie Mae Flores** 77t, **Gideon Rey Salcedo** 104, **Haron Deo Vargas** 14b, 147tb, **Imelda Luna** 80, **Jake Wilson Binaday** 48b, 51, 79, 86r, 88t, 88mr, 116, 118, 135, 138tr, 140b, 153t, **Jamie Ann Dichaves** 12t, 13t, 14t, **Jan van der Ploeg** 88ml, **Jason Apolonio** 60t, 64b, 82, 89b, 112, 149tlr, **Jasper Leif P. Maypa** 146, **Joe Merfurt N. Lama** 17, 26b, 31tr, 35, 138tl, **John Alaban** 111t, **John Lester Bibar** 139b, **Jay Paul E Mantuon** 26t, **John Rey Callado** 53b, 127, 130, **Jojo De Peralta** 20t, 37, 108, 117, 125t, 138b, 145, 156, **Justine Magbanua** 56b, 100, 161ml, **Kaila Ledesma** 148t, **Kier Mitchel Pitogo** 58b, 73t, **Kirk A. Cabello** 55b, **Kristian James Suetos** 162t, **Lief Erikson Gamalo** 92, 102br, **Lim Bryan Kutat** 149b, **Ma. Niña R. Quibod** 151, **Maren Gaulke** 41tb, 43b, 50tb, 52b, 53t, 61tb, 63b, 66b, 75, 111b, 120, 132tb, **Marvin Cascante** 136t, **Meljory D. Corvera** 134b, 161br, **Melody Joy Dagta** 72b, **Merlijn van Weerd** 62t, **Niel C. Jarina** 31tm, **Niño Caguimbal** 102t, 160, **Othoniel E. Calago** 121, **Paul Henric Gojo Cruz** 59b, 66t, 98b, 153b, **Peter John Cacayan** 105, **Peter Widmann** 63t, 142, **Philip C. Baltazar** 18b, 141, **Pol Cariño** 52t, **Rachel Casio** 30b, **Rai Gomez** 115b, **Rhett Arthur Diana** 12b, **Roderick Parcon** 72t, 115t, 123, **Ronaldo Lagat** 103, **Ronny Boos** 62b, 69, 109t, **Russell Evan Venturina** 30t, **Shameer Gappal Mangkabong** 58t, **Shekainah Alaban** 114, **Stefanie Grace Ang** 139t, **Tony Gerard** 93tb, 95, 119t, 154b, **Tristan Luap P. Senarillos** 33, 67, 113, 161bl, **Virgilio Gales** 84, **Wilhelm Tan** 29, **Wojtek Nieszporek** 85, 86l, 109b, **Yñigo del Prado** 18t, 19b, 25, 65b, 73b, 88br, 89t, 98t, 106, 124, 126, 140t, 144, 158br.

Great care has been taken to maintain the accuracy of the information contained in this work. However, neither the publishers nor the authors can be held responsible for any consequences arising from the use of the information contained therein.

ISBN 978-1-912081-56-1

Edited by Krystyna Mayer
Designed by Gulmohur Press, New Delhi
Printed and bound in Malaysia by Times Offset (M) Sdn. Bhd.

MIX
Paper | Supporting
responsible forestry
FSC® C001507
www.fsc.org

·CONTENTS·

INTRODUCTION

The Philippines is an archipelagic country with 7,641 islands. It is situated south-east of mainland Asia and has a land area of approximately 300,000km2. It is one of the world's 17 most mega-biodiverse countries, but is also identified as one of the 25 biodiversity hotspot countries due to having the most threatened wildlife. As currently understood, 371 indigenous reptile taxa are known to occur in the country, with a high level of endemism (78.7 per cent). In addition, seven non-native reptiles have been documented in the Philippines. The herpetofaunal diversity is expected to increase significantly in the coming years, since ongoing taxonomic studies continuously describe new species to science.

CLIMATE

The climate in the Philippines is characterized by high temperatures (average 21°C–32°C), high relative humidity (average 71–85 per cent), and pronounced wet (June–November) and dry (December–May) seasons. Annually, about 20 tropical cyclones pass through the Philippines and cause severe damage to the environment, agricultural crops and properties.

BIOGEOGRAPHICAL REGIONS

Various geological processes starting in the Mesozoic Era influenced the distribution of wildlife in the Philippines. The repeated sea-level fluctuations during the Pleistocene Epoch, particularly in the last ice age, 15,000–20,000 years ago, resulted in numerous formations and fragmentations of islands. Nearby islands became connected when the sea level was 100–140m lower than it is in the present day, and formed contiguous larger land masses known as Pleistocene Aggregate Island Complexes (PAICs). In the absence of marine dispersal barriers, this phenomenon facilitated the spread of species to previously inaccessible land areas.

The Philippines comprises five major zoogeographical or faunal regions, namely Luzon (including Polillo, Marinduque and Catanduanes), Palawan (including Balabac, Busuanga, Calauit, Coron, Culion and Dumaran), West Visayas (including Cebu, Masbate, Negros and Panay), Mindanao (including Basilan, Bohol, Dinagat, Leyte, Samar and Siargao) and Sulu Archipelago (including Jolo and Tawi-Tawi). Recent studies have highlighted that the distribution and diversification of reptiles in the Philippines are more dynamic and complex than previously thought. Several sub-faunal regions that may or may not have been previously connected with nearby major islands are increasingly recognized as important areas for conservation due to having a microendemic or unique subset of herpetofauna: 1. Batanes, 2. Babuyan, 3. Mindoro, 4. Bicol Peninsula of southern Luzon Island, 5. Romblon (including Tablas and Sibuyan), 6. East Visayas (Samar, Leyte and Biliran), 7. Zamboanga Peninsula of western Mindanao, and 8. Turtle Islands (north-east of Borneo).

Habitats

Reptiles utilize various habitats and microhabitats. Many adaptable species of gecko, sun skink, water monitor lizard and snake tolerate and thrive in urban areas and other heavily disturbed habitats, but most species require somewhat intact forests to thrive. Coastal areas also host numerous reptiles such as sea turtles, sea kraits, sea snakes, and a few gecko and skink species.

National Legislation

The Philippines has strong laws in place for the protection and conservation of wildlife and other natural resources. The Department of Environment and Natural Resources (DENR) is the main governmental agency mandated to implement the Republic Act No. 9147, otherwise known as the Wildlife Resources Conservation and Protection Act. The law prohibits killing, inflicting injury, introducing, trading, collecting, hunting, possessing, maltreating or transporting of wildlife without permits. Violations of the Act may be punishable by up to 12 years imprisonment and/or a PHP 1,000,000 (USD 17,856) fine. In Palawan Province, the Palawan Council for Sustainable Development (PCDS) is mandated to implement the Republic Act No. 7611 or the Strategic Environmental Plan for Palawan Act.

Conservation

The Philippine herpetofauna is facing various threats to its survival, including habitat loss and fragmentation, climate change, introduced species and the illegal wildlife trade. Researchers from the government, academia and non-governmental organizations are working collaboratively and/or independently to identify threats and come up with pragmatic solutions for the protection and conservation of the Philippines' reptiles. The Philippine wildlife authority (Department Administrative Order 2019-09) and the International Union for Conservation of Nature (IUCN) Red List of Threatened Species (version 2022-02) assessed 14 and 38 reptile species as threatened respectively. Readers are encouraged to consult the IUCN Red List website at www.iucnredlist.org for the latest assessment.

Where to Look for Reptiles

In tropical countries such as the Philippines, reptiles are some of the most conspicuous faunal groups you can encounter. House geckos are ever present in man-made structures, while some highly tolerant to modified environment reptiles, such as water monitor lizards and snakes, may be seen in nature parks and on river banks in urban areas. Visits to national parks or protected areas are necessary to see forest-obligate species. If you wish to visit these, always contact the national park administrator, by phone or email, before making a trip to confirm the permit requirements, fees, operating hours, available transport and accommodation, local weather conditions and security concerns.

IDENTIFICATION

Some species can be easily identified by their colour and pattern, while others require a more thorough examination such as scale counting and measurement in the laboratory. Aside from examining physical characters, it is also helpful to note the general habitat, microhabitat, time of observation, location (island) and behaviour of a species you are trying to identify.

TOPOGRAPHY

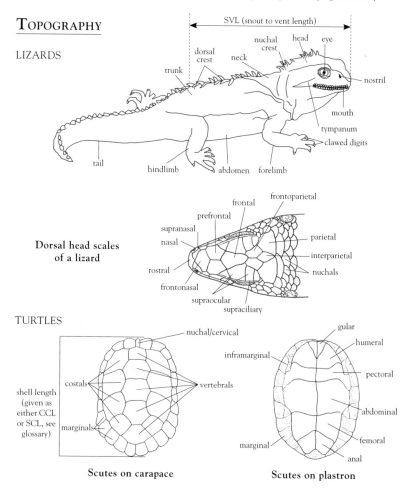

LIZARDS

Dorsal head scales of a lizard

TURTLES

Scutes on carapace

Scutes on plastron

SNAKES

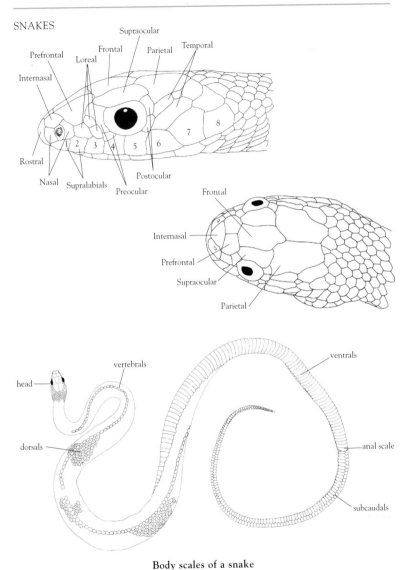

Body scales of a snake

SNAKEBITE

The reptile assemblage of the Philippines includes highly venomous snakes both on the land and in the sea. The best way to avoid being bitten by a snake is to keep an appropriate distance from it. Avoid handling snakes, even non-venomous species. Seek medical care immediately if snakebite occurs. The Research Institute for Tropical Medicine (RITM) produces antivenom derived from the venom of the Northern Philippine Cobra. More recently, a private pharmaceutical company started to produce a polyvalent antivenom derived from the venom of the Southern and Northern Philippine Cobras and King Cobra (Mindanao). There are no available antivenoms for pitvipers *Trimeresurus* spp., *Tropidolaemus* spp., sea snakes *Hydrophis* spp. or sea kraits *Laticauda* spp. in the Philippines.

ABOUT THIS BOOK

The aim of this book is to provide introductory information on reptiles occurring in the Philippines. At least 170 out of 378 taxa (45 per cent) are described and illustrated. A few reptiles with uncertain taxonomy and/or distribution (such as *Gonocephalus* species) are included to draw the attention of readers to the ongoing studies of taxonomists and systematists. There are several ways of assessing the sizes of reptiles. In the case of turtles and terrapins, in this book the curved carapace length (CCL) is given for sea turtles, the straight carapace length (SCL) for other turtles. In lizards, size is generally determined by measuring the body length from snout to vent (SVL). Many lizards may lose, then regenerate the tail, so knowledge of total length from snout to tail (TL) is of little use for identification purposes. Total length (TL) is generally used for snakes. See p. 6 for illustrations. In this book, only the TL or SVL measurement is available for some species of lizard and snake, in which case either measurement may be given. In some instances, both the SVL and TL measurements are available, and both are given. Distribution by island, and brief ecological information are provided for each featured species. Photographs of juveniles that are distinctly different from adults are provided where available. See also checklist of reptiles of the Philippines (p. 163).

GLOSSARY

anterior Oriented towards front.
arboreal Living above the ground or in trees, vegetation or rocks.
autotomy Ability of a species to break off a body part, usually the tail, when threatened or stressed.
asl Above sea level.
carnivore Organism that predates on animals.
caudal Refers to tail or towards tail region.
CCL (curved carapace length) Measurement following curve of carapace from anterior to posterior.
clutch Set of eggs laid by a female at one time.
crepuscular Active during dusk and dawn.
dewlap Skin-flap under throat of certain lizards; also called gular pouch.
digit Finger or toe.
distal Further away from point of origin.
diurnal Active during day time.
dorsal Towards upper surface of an animal.

dorsum Upper side of an animal.

endemic Refers to species occurring only in a restricted geographical region or country.

fossorial Living underground or burrowing.

frontal Large median scale located on top of head and between eyes.

frugivore Animal that consumes mainly fruits.

gular fold Transverse fold of skin on throat.

hervibore Animal that consumes plants.

imbricate Feature wherein adjacent edges of scales are overlapping.

introduced species Refers to species accidentally or intentionally brought into an area where it does not naturally occur; also known as non-native or exotic.

keeled Refers to ridge/ridges on scales.

labial Pertaining to lip.

lamella (pl. **lamellae**) Transverse pad underneath digits of lizards.

lateral Pertaining to side of a body part.

nape Back of neck.

nasal Scale on side of head containing nostril opening.

native Refers to species occurring naturally in a geographical region; also known as indigenous.

nocturnal Active during night time.

nuchal Back of neck.

ocellus (pl. **ocelli**) Rounded, eye-like spot.

omnivore Animal that consumes both plants and animals.

oviparous Laying eggs.

ovoviviparous Reproduction by retaining fertilized eggs within female's body and eventually giving birth to live young.

parthenogenesis Mode of reproduction when an egg develops into an embryo without fertilization of sperm.

patagium (pl. **patagia**) Extended skin between front and back limbs, serving as wing in gliding animals.

piscivore Animal that predates on fish.

posterior Oriented towards back.

preanal/precloacal Situated in front of anal opening or cloacal region.

preocular Anterior to eye.

primary forest Undisturbed natural forest.

proximal Close to point of origin.

rostral Scale at tip of snout.

SCL (straight carapace length) Measurement of a carapace in straight line.

scute Thickened horny or bony plate on turtle's shell or back of crocodile.

secondary forest Previously disturbed forest with new natural growth.

species complex Closely related group of species.

subcaudal Underside or ventral surface of tail.

supranasal Scale above nasal.

SVL (snout–vent length) Measurement from snout-tip to anal opening in straight line.

sympatric Refers to species occurring in same area at the same time.

terrestrial Living on surface of the ground.

TL (total length) Measurement from snout-tip to tail-tip in straight line.

tubercle Nodule on surface of skin.

tympanum Eardrum.

ventral Towards underside of an animal.

CROCODYLIDAE (CROCODILES)
The 18 crocodile species are spread throughout the world and live in or near waterbodies. All species are carnivorous and individuals occasionally predate on large mammals.

Philippine Crocodile ▪ *Crocodylus mindorensis* TL 3m ⓔ

DESCRIPTION The smaller of the two native crocodiles in the Philippines, this species can be distinguished by its maximum size of 3m TL and presence of 4–6 (usually six) enlarged post-occipital scales. Dorsal colour grey to olive with black oblong spots. Ventral scale rows: 22–26. Females smaller than males. **DISTRIBUTION** Dalupiri (extirpated?), Luzon, Mindanao, Siargao (introduced). **HABITS AND HABITAT** Floats in water or basks by day. Inhabits mangroves and freshwater habitats such as rivers, creeks, lakes and marshes. Juveniles feed on insects, shrimps, snails and small vertebrates. Larger individuals feed on fish, reptiles, birds and mammals. Females construct mound nests on dry riverbanks and lay 16–33 eggs per clutch. Naturally incubated eggs hatch in 65–78 days. Average hatchling size 250mm TL and weight 60g. **NOTE** One of the most Critically Endangered crocodiles in the world, with estimated population size of fewer than 100 adult individuals, due to freshwater wetland habitat destruction and persecution.

Saltwater Crocodile ▪ *Crocodylus porosus* TL 7m

DESCRIPTION Largest extant reptile in the world, attaining up to 7m TL and 1,200kg in weight. Head large and elongated, with pair of ridges from front of eyes to tip of snout. Dorsal body, limbs and tail brown to grey with black spots. Ventral scale rows: 29–34. Short limbs muscular with webbed digits. **DISTRIBUTION** Balabac, Catanduanes, Languyan, Luzon, Mindanao, Palawan, Siargao, Tawi-Tawi. **HABITS AND HABITAT** Semi-aquatic and nocturnal. Inhabits sea coasts and freshwater habitats such as rivers, lakes, marshes, swamps, creeks and streams. Females construct nest mounds in wetlands and lay up to 90 eggs per clutch. Incubation period 80–90 days.

CHELONIIDAE (SEA TURTLES)
All sea turtles inhabit marine environments, but return to land to lay eggs. Elongated, flipper-like front limbs allow them to swim gracefully in water, but make movement on land awkward. While they can remain submerged underwater for more than an hour, they still need to swim to the surface to breathe air. The survival of several species is threatened due to widespread poaching of turtles for curios and eggs for food.

Green Sea Turtle ▪ *Chelonia mydas* CCL 1,250mm

DESCRIPTION Typical carapace brown or olive with or without markings. Head moderate in size with one pair of prefrontals. Five vertebral scutes and four lateral scutes on each side. One claw on anterior side of forelimb. Hatchlings have black carapace and white plastron; carapace and limbs have white margin. **DISTRIBUTION** Widespread, including on Baguan, Catanduanes, Dinagat, Leyte, Luzon, Mapun, Masbate, Mindanao, Mindoro, Negros, Palawan, Panay, Panikian, Samar, Siargao, Spratly, Taganak, Tawi-Tawi. **HABITS AND HABITAT** Aquatic and herbivorous. Inhabits shallow lagoons, feeding on seagrasses and algae. Adult females nest 1–5 times per season and lay average of up to 130 eggs per clutch. Egg size 40–46mm in diameter. High nesting aggregations occur in southwestern Philippines. **NOTE** Illegal collection of turtles and eggs is one of the biggest threats to its survival.

Hatchling

Adult

Pacific Hawksbill Sea Turtle ■ *Eretmochelys imbricata bissa*
CCL 910mm

DESCRIPTION Marine turtle with prominent hooked beak. Carapace brown with dark irregular markings. Five vertebral scutes and four overlapping lateral scutes on each side. Carapace margin serrated posteriorly. Head moderate in size with two pairs of prefrontals. Two claws on anterior side of forelimb. Carapaces and plastrons of hatchlings black. **DISTRIBUTION** Widespread, including on Baguan, Bohol, Leyte, Luzon, Marinduque, Mindanao, Mindoro, Negros, Palawan, Panay. **HABITS AND HABITAT** Aquatic and spongivore. Inhabits shallow, coral-strewn habitats. Feeds mainly on sponges, but also consumes algae and coral anemones. Females lay 70–180 eggs per clutch. Egg size 32–36mm in diameter.

Hatchling

Adult

Olive Ridley Sea Turtle ■ *Lepidochelys olivacea* CCL 700mm

DESCRIPTION Carapace smooth and olive in colour. Seven vertebral scutes and 6–9 lateral scutes on each side, which can be asymmetrical. Head olive above, pale yellow below and with two pairs of prefrontals. Two claws on anterior side of forelimb. Hatchlings dark grey (black when wet), with three prominent dorsal keels. **DISTRIBUTION** Luzon, Mindanao, Mindoro, Negros, Palawan, Tablas. **HABITS AND HABITAT** Diurnal and omnivorous. Inhabits warm marine environments, feeding on crabs, shrimps, lobsters, urchins, fish, jellyfish and algae. Females lay 105–120 eggs per clutch in grey sandy beaches near rivers, lagoons or estuaries. Spherical egg 37–42mm in diameter.

Hatchling

Adult

> **DERMOCHELYIDAE (LEATHERBACK SEA TURTLE)**
> This is the largest living turtle in the world, with a leathery skin on the carapace. It inhabits marine environments and feeds mainly on jellyfish. The family consists of the only remaining living species.

Leatherback Sea Turtle ▪ *Dermochelys coriacea* CCL 1.7m

DESCRIPTION Largest and heaviest extant turtle, measuring close to 2m CCL and weighing up to 600kg. Easily identifiable, with its leathery carapace with seven longitudinal ridges. Dorsal colour dark grey with white spots. Pair of large forelimbs without scales or claws. **DISTRIBUTION** Catanduanes, Guimaras, Leyte, Luzon, Mindoro, Negros, Palawan, Panay, Samar. **HABITS AND HABITAT** Diurnal and aquatic. Usually found in open ocean foraging on jellyfish. Females lay 60–120 eggs per clutch on isolated beaches adjacent to deep water. Egg 51–55mm in diameter. Less than five nesting sites identified in the Philippines.

> **Emydidae (New World Pond Turtles)**
> A diverse semi-aquatic freshwater turtle family in the Americas and Europe, several species are popular in the pet trade and bred in captivity in large quantities. Two species, *Trachemys scripta* and *Chrysemys picta*, have established feral populations in the Philippines.

Red-eared Slider ▪ *Trachemys scripta elegans* SCL 300mm

DESCRIPTION Juveniles of this attractive species have bright green carapace with yellow markings. Head adorned with narrow yellow stripes and prominent red stripe behind eye on each side. Plastron yellow with blotches. Adult males have elongated foreclaws. Colour becomes dull brown or grey and darker with age. Listed as one of 100 worst invasive species in the world, and escapees and feral populations have been documented in the Philippines. **DISTRIBUTION** Cebu, Luzon, Mindanao. **HABITS AND HABITAT** Diurnal, semi-aquatic and omnivorous. Usually seen basking on riverbanks and logs, and in artificial ponds. Courtship and mating occur in water. Females lay up to 25 eggs per clutch. Incubation period 65–75 days under natural conditions.

> **GEOEMYDIDAE (OLD WORLD POND TURTLES)**
> Semi-aquatic turtles with widespread distribution in Asia (subfamily Geoemydinae) and South America (subfamily Rhinoclemmydinae). The family is currently represented by two subfamilies, 19 genera and 71 species. Four genera, *Cuora*, *Cyclemys*, *Heosemys* and *Siebenrockiella*, occur in the Philippines.

Philippine Box Turtle (e)

▪ *Cuora philippinensis* SCL 170mm

DESCRIPTION Common and widely distributed species. Carapace dark brown and smooth. Head moderate, and dark brown above and pale yellow below. Pair of pale yellow stripes above eyes runs from snout to neck. Snout projected, with slightly hooked upper jaw. Plastron yellowish-brown, with or without dark blotches. **DISTRIBUTION** Bohol, Cagraray, Camiguin Norte, Cebu, Dinagat, Fuga, Guimaras, Leyte, Luzon, Marinduque, Masbate, Mindanao, Mindoro, Negros, Pan de Azucar, Panay, Polillo, Samar, Semirara, Sibuyan, Tablas, Verde. **HABITS AND HABITAT** Diurnal and semi-aquatic. Inhabits streams, rivers, shallow lakes, ponds and flooded rice fields. Feeds on vegetation, invertebrates and opportunistically on small vertebrates. Females lay 1–2 eggs per clutch. Eggs elongated, brittle and measure 48–57 x 27–31mm. Incubation at 28°–29°C takes 74–78 days to hatch. Hatchling size 38–48mm SCL and weight 12–18g. **NOTE** Species heavily poached for pet trade.

Asian Leaf Turtle ■ *Cyclemys dentata* SCL 220mm

DESCRIPTION Oval carapace light to dark brown and distinctly flat on top. Median carapacial keel and pair of lateral keels wear down with age. Nuchal scute longer than wide. Marginal scutes: 11–12; serrated posteriorly and very prominent in juveniles. Five vertebral scutes, with second to fifth broader than long. Head moderate in size and can

retract completely. Snout slightly projected. Dorsal of head has black dots. Brown stripes on neck and lower jaw. Plastron yellowish-brown with dark radiating lines on scutes. **DISTRIBUTION** Balabac, Palawan, Siasi, Tawi-Tawi. **HABITS AND HABITAT** Semi-aquatic and omnivorous, inhabiting shallow streams and ponds. Feeds on vegetation, fruits, crustaceans, fish and carrion. Clutch size 2–3 elongated and brittle-shelled eggs. Average hatchling size 56mm SCL.

Tawi-Tawi

Palawan

Philippine Forest Turtle ▪ *Siebenrockiella leytensis* SCL 300mm ⓔ

DESCRIPTION Carapace brown to dark brown. Nuchal scute present; 11–13 marginal and five vetebral scutes; second to fourth gingko leaf shaped. Head large with slightly hooked and bicuspid upper jaw. White or yellowish transverse band on top of head. Plastron light yellowish-brown with or without dark brown blotches. Gular scutes (first pair) large and with prominent notch in between. Anal scutes (last pair) rounded or 'V' shaped.

Hatchlings have pair of orange spots on lower jaw; carapace margin serrated posteriorly. **DISTRIBUTION** Dumaran, Palawan. **HABITS AND HABITAT** Semi-aquatic, inhabiting streams, rivers, swamps and lakes in primary and secondary forests at near sea level to 300m asl. Also seen in flooded rice fields bordering forests. Active at night, foraging for fish, crabs, shrimps, snails and fruits. Females lay 1–2 oblong, brittle-shelled eggs per clutch. Eggs 41–58mm long x 20–29mm wide, and weigh 18–30g. Hatchlings 41–43mm SCL. **NOTE** Poaching for pet trade the biggest threat to survival of species in the wild.

Hatchling

Adult

> ### TRIONYCHIDAE (SOFTSHELL TURTLES)
> Primarily aquatic species with flattened carapace covered with leathery skin and inhabiting freshwater habitats. Softshell turtles have a long neck, a prominent proboscis on the snout and extensive webbing between digits.

Malayan Softshell Turtle ▪ *Dogania subplana* SCL 310mm

DESCRIPTION Carapace oval, flat and with parallel sides; colour olive to brown, with black medial stripe and 2–3 pairs of small black spots. Head wider than long neck. Proboscis long. Thin black line from front of eye to snout. Immature individuals have

deep orange blotch behind each eye to side of head that fades with age. Plastron off-white. Males have thicker and longer tail than females. **DISTRIBUTION** Palawan. **HABITS AND HABITAT** Primarily aquatic, feeding on fish, shrimps, crabs, snails and fruits. Occurs in forest streams and slow-flowing rivers. **NOTE** Records outside Palawan faunal region might be of misidentified Chinese Softshell Turtle (opposite).

Asian Giant Softshell Turtle ▪ *Pelochelys cantorii* SCL 1,000mm

DESCRIPTION Very large softshell turtle with small head and short proboscis. Carapace flat and surrounded by soft, cartilaginous margins posteriorly. Carapace olive; plastron off-white without markings. **DISTRIBUTION** Luzon, Mindanao. **HABITS AND HABITAT**

Highly aquatic species that rarely leaves the water. Usually seen when accidentally caught by fishermen using hooks and lines. Primarily carnivorous, predating on fish, shrimps, crabs and snails, but also consumes plant matter. Inhabits lakes, rivers and occasionally sea coasts. **NOTE** Populations in the Philippines might be a distinct species.

Chinese Softshell Turtle ■ *Pelodiscus sinensis* SCL 260mm

DESCRIPTION Introduced species in the Philippines. Carapace longer than broad, smooth, olive to brown, and with blunt tubercles on anterior rim above neck. Eyes close to top of head, proboscis long, and neck narrow and long. Plastron cream, with or without dark blotches. Carapaces of immature individuals have short ridges. Carapaces of hatchlings almost round; plastrons deep orange. **DISTRIBUTION** Bohol, Catanduanes,

Cebu, Leyte, Luzon, Marinduque, Mindanao, Mindoro, Negros, Panay, Tablas. **HABITS AND HABITAT** Defensive turtle that readily bites when handled. Inhabits natural rivers, lakes, swamps, man-made ponds, lakes and canals, and flooded rice fields. Feeds on fish, shrimps, crabs, snails and plant matter. Females lay 15–28 eggs per clutch 2–4 times a year. Eggs white, spherical and about 20mm in diameter. Eggs incubated at 28°–32°C hatch in 45–50 days. Average hatchling 27mm SCL.

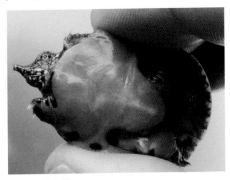

Plastron of hatchling

Juvenile

> ## AGAMIDAE (AGAMIDS)
> This is a diverse diurnal lizard family with 560 species occurring in a range of habitats from rainforests to open areas. Many species are adorned with spiny crests and long tails. Agamids feed mainly on anthropods, but several species are herbivores.

Green Crested Lizard ∎ *Bronchocela cristatella* SVL 136mm; TL 469mm

DESCRIPTION Species complex occuring in major faunal regions. Primarily bright green, but can quickly change to brown or grey when threatened or stressed. Low crest from neck to dorsal area. Head wedge shaped with moderate-sized, dark brown ear-openings. Large gular sac in adult males extending to anterior of forelimbs. Limbs and digits slender and long. Tail very long, 3.4 times SVL. **DISTRIBUTION** Bohol, Cebu, Jolo, Palawan, Panay, Masbate, Mindanao, Mindoro, Negros, Samar. **HABITS AND HABITAT** Diurnal and arboreal, inhabiting lowland primary and secondary forests, but thrives in disturbed areas such as parks and gardens at sea level to 1,200m asl. Often seen on low hedges basking by day. Females typically lay two spindle-shaped eggs per clutch. Hatchlings 35–36.5mm SVL. **NOTE** Taxonomic review needed to delimit species distribution and identify new species in genus.

Marbled Crested Lizard ■ *Bronchocela marmorata*
SVL 125mm; TL 550mm (e)

DESCRIPTION Agamid lizard with laterally compressed body, long, slender limbs, and very long tail, 3.3 times SVL. Nuchal crest pointing upwards, and higher than dorsal crest. Upper body scale rows: 0–2, pointing upwards. Moderate gular sac in adult males. Tympanum well developed. Scales on dorsum keeled. When relaxed, colour is green, but can quickly turn to grey or brown when stressed. There may be diagonal markings on body. Ventral scales strongly keeled. **DISTRIBUTION** Catanduanes, Lahuy, Luzon, Mindoro, Polillo. **HABITS AND HABITAT** Diurnal and arboreal. Often seen basking on low vegetation in the morning. Females lay two spindle-shaped eggs per clutch.

Common Garden Lizard ■ *Calotes versicolor* SVL 100mm

DESCRIPTION Colour variable – light brown, yellowish-brown or grey. Head triangular in profile with well-developed tympanum. Nuchal crest moderate and higher than dorsal crest. Keeled scales on dorsum. Tail very long, almost three times SVL. Introduced species in the Philippines. **DISTRIBUTION** Luzon (Cavite, Laguna, NCR, Rizal). **HABITS AND HABITAT** Diurnal and arboreal. Seen on trees, shrubs and empty lots overgrown with vegetation in urban areas. Feeds on invertebrates such as crickets, grasshoppers, cockroaches and spiders. Females lay up to 15 eggs per clutch and can produce several clutches per season.

Adult

Hatchling

Green Flying Lizard ▪ *Draco cyanopterus* SVL 95mm ⓔ

DESCRIPTION Active, arboreal agamid with small head and slender body. Pair of enlarged, thorn-like scales above eyes. Dorsal body grey, tan or brown. Patagium supported by six ribs. Dorsal patagium has large, yellowish-green patches between ribs (males), or dark reticulation or mottling over peach or orange base colour. Triangular dewlap in males reddish-brown with yellowish to orange tip. Tail has dark brown bands. **DISTRIBUTION** Camiguin Sur, Dinagat, Mindanao, Siargao. **HABITS AND HABITAT** Diurnal; often seen on tree trunks in open areas such as coconut grooves and forest edges, foraging principally on ants.

Günther's Flying Lizard
■ *Draco guentheri* SVL 97mm

DESCRIPTION Colour of dorsal patagium dark green with yellowish-green or bluish spots (males), or black with grey wash and reddish or orange spots (females). Triangular dewlap of males immaculate green or white, with yellow tip. Six ribs supporting patagium. Enlarged, thorn-like scale above eye. Females larger (SVL 97mm) than males (SVL 85mm). Tail light grey with dark brown bars. **DISTRIBUTION** Basilan, Bongao, Jolo, Mindanao, Sanga-Sanga, Siasi, Simunul. **HABITS AND HABITAT** Diurnal and arboreal. Occurs in secondary forests and forest edges in western Mindanao, particularly Zamboanga Peninsula. Often seen on coconut trees while foraging for ants by day.

Male

Female

Palawan Flying Lizard ■ *Draco palawanensis* SVL 84mm ⓔ

DESCRIPTION Dorsal pattern brown; black and tan pigments with pale grey base colour, giving mottled appearance. Tail banded with dark brown and pale grey. Males and females have melanic interorbital spot, with only females also having melanic nuchal spot. Females have radiating melanic lines in orbital region. Gular pattern in males brown mottled on pale tan base colour, with one-third of dewlap appearing grey-brown. Dewlap appears orange during display. Dorsal patagial dull orange with several pale longitudinal striations. Distinguished from other *Draco* species by unique patagial colour pattern of dull orange or yellow, with rectangular black spots increasing in size near patagial margin. **DISTRIBUTION** Palawan. **HABITS AND HABITAT** Like other *Draco* species, males often seen displaying dewlap and patagia while doing push-up movement with front legs. Common on trunks of coconut and *Casuarina* trees, and often found in heavily disturbed habitats. Otherwise occurs in dipterocarp rainforests, in edges or canopies.

Reticulated Flying Lizard ■ *Draco reticulatus* SVL 91mm ⓔ

DESCRIPTION Dorsal patagium dark brown to black with large, pale yellow or orange spots. Large dewlap of males triangular and reddish-brown, with pale white spots proximally and yellowish-brown distally. Enlarged, thorn-like scale above eye. Patagium supported by six ribs. Eye region of males encircled by black colour. Tail grey with brown bars. **DISTRIBUTION** Bohol, Lapinin Chico, Leyte, Samar. **HABITS AND HABITAT** Diurnal and arboreal. Occurs in forests, forest edges and open areas with ample sunlight. Common in coconut groves. Feeds primarily on ants.

Luzon Flying Lizard ▪ *Draco spilopterus* SVL 103mm; TL 234mm

DESCRIPTION Species complex with at least four lineages. Dorsal patagium yellowish-orange with small brown spots (males) or dark brown with or without pale yellow mottling (females). Enlarged, thorn-like scale above eye absent. Patagium supported by six ribs. Females larger (103mm SVL) than males (90mm SVL). Males have triangular, yellow or white dewlap. Dorsal body pale brown in both sexes. **DISTRIBUTION** Bantayan, Boracay, Carabao, Catanduanes, Cebu, Guimaras, Inampulugan, Kalotkot, Lubang, Luzon, Marinduque, Masbate, Negros, Panay, Polillo, Siquijor. **HABITS AND HABITAT** Diurnal and arboreal. Commonly seen in forests along trails with ample sunlight, and coconut plantations. Feeds mainly on ants on tree trunks, but may also forage on or near the ground.

Mindanao (south-east)

Forest lizards ■ *Gonocephalus* spp.
SVL 88–105mm; TL 228–280mm ⓔ

DESCRIPTION Three species currently recognized in the Philippines (G. *interruptus*, G. *semperi* and G. *sophiae*), but they are taxonomically confused. Recent study hypothesized up to eight lineages throughout the archipelago. Head triangular in profile. Nuchal crest well developed and much higher than dorsal crest. Body laterally compressed. Dorsum green to brown with markings. Tail has dark bands. **DISTRIBUTION** Widespread except Palawan. **HABITS AND HABITAT** Diurnal and arboreal. Inhabits riparian habitats in primary and secondary lowland forests, often on small tree trunks 1–3m above the ground.

Negros

Luzon

Cebu

Mindoro

Mindanao (south-west)

Sibuyan

Philippine Sailfin Lizard ▪ *Hydrosaurus pustulatus*
SVL 288mm; TL 990mm ⓔ

DESCRIPTION Large, brown to green sailfin lizard. High sail of up to 8cm on anterior part of tail, which is more prominent on male than female and used as a propeller when swimming. Crest runs along neck and dorsal area. Digits long and relatively large to aid

movement on water. **DISTRIBUTION** Bohol, Camiguin Sur, Catanduanes, Catonavan, Cebu, Dinagat, Leyte, Luzon, Mindanao, Mindoro, Negros, Panay, Polillo, Romblon, Samar, Tablas. **HABITS AND HABITAT** Primarily diurnal and herbivorous. Strong swimmer that can run on the water's surface on its hindlegs for short distances when threatened. Lives in various lowland habitats such as mangroves, coastal forests, and banks of forest streams and rivers. Oviparous, laying 2–8 eggs per clutch.

Juvenile

Adult

Annulated Bent-toed Gecko ■ *Cyrtodactylus annulatus* SVL 81mm ⓔ

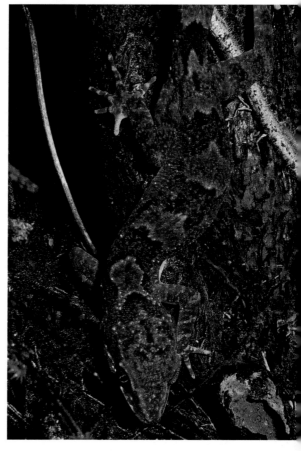

DESCRIPTION Dorsum light greyish-brown overall, with 4–5 irregularly shaped, dark transverse markings and conical or pointed tubercles. Light grey superciliaries. Lower labials: 7–10, upper labials: 7–8. Dark brown stripe from snout through eye to nape, and dark 'M' marking on neck. Limbs and digits banded; 17–22 lamellae beneath fourth toe. Six precloacal pores arranged in inverted 'V' in males, and femoral pore-bearing scales lacking. Postcloacal tubercles on each side: 2–4. Tail has light and dark transverse bands; dark bands on original tail broader than light bands posteriorly. **DISTRIBUTION** Bohol, Camiguin Sur, Cebu, Inampulugan, Leyte, Mindanao, Ponson, Pacijan, Siquijor. **HABITS AND HABITAT** Nocturnal and arboreal. Commonly found on tree trunks and under rotting logs on forest floors in riparian habitats near streams. Females lay two eggs per clutch. Hatchling 25–28mm SVL.

Leyte Bent-toed Gecko ■ *Cyrtodactylus gubaot* SVL 100mm e

DESCRIPTION Dorsum light brown with medium to dark brown markings. Dark marking on nape 'V' shaped or triangular. Upper labials: 9–10, lower labials: 7–8. Mid-body transverse row of tubercles: 18–20. Ventral dark grey with black markings. Lamellae beneath fourth toe: 24–30. Tail has transverse bands that become darker posteriorly. **DISTRIBUTION** Leyte. **HABITS AND HABITAT** Nocturnal and arboreal. Inhabits primary to heavily disturbed forests in riparian habitats near streams. Commonly seen on tree trunks and boulders.

Jambangan Bent-toed Gecko ■ *Cyrtodactylus jambangan* SVL 82mm ⓔ

DESCRIPTION Dorsum uniform light greyish-brown with round brown spots and irregular markings. 'V'-shaped marking on nape. Bright yellow superciliaries. Broad brown postocular stripe may extend beyond shoulder. Body tubercles larger and denser on posterior and lateral region. Lamellae: 20–24 beneath fourth toe. Males have two rows of enlarged pore-bearing scales on precloacal region. Femoral pores absent in both sexes. Tail has moderately broad transverse brown bands.

DISTRIBUTION Basilan, Bitinan, Buban, Bongao, Cancuman, Dipolod, Great Sta Cruz, Jolo, Mindanao, Tamuk, Tawi-Tawi, Teipono.

HABITS AND HABITAT Nocturnal and arboreal. Occurs in low to mid-elevation forests in riparian habitats near streams. Usually seen on tree trunks and rocks on rivers or stream banks.

Philippine Bent-toed Gecko ■ *Cyrtodactylus philippinicus* SVL 98mm

DESCRIPTION Dorsum light yellowish-brown overall, with five irregularly shaped, dark transverse bands on body. Upper labials: 6–10, lower labials: 5–8. Dark 'M' marking on nape; 19–26 lamellae beneath fourth toe; 8–12 precloacal pore-bearing scales; 2–5 postcloacal tubercles on each side. Tail tapering, with light and dark transverse bands. **DISTRIBUTION** Luzon, Panay. **HABITS AND HABITAT** Nocturnal and arboreal. Commonly seen on tree trunks close to forest floor. Found at sea level to 1,100m asl in riparian habitats. Female lays two eggs per clutch. Hatchlings 30–35mm SVL.

Palawan Bent-toed Gecko ■ *Cyrtodactylus redimiculus* SVL 94mm

DESCRIPTION Dorsum overall dark brown with reticulated pattern on head and nape, and 3–4 narrow, light brown transverse bands on body. Upper labials: 7–11, lower labials: 6–8. Dark brown superciliaries. Dorsal body has 18–22 rows of paravertebral tubercles. No ventrolateral fold on body. Beneath fourth toe, 19–24 lamellae; 5–8 preanal pores and 8–9 femoral pores in males; 4–6 postcloacal tubercles. Tail dark brown with narrower white transverse bands. **DISTRIBUTION** Palawan. **HABITS AND HABITAT** Nocturnal and arboreal. Inhabits riparian habitats of forests at 300–800m asl.

Tender-skinned Gecko ▪ *Gehyra mutilata* SVL 60mm

DESCRIPTION The only known *Gehyra* species in the Philippines with moderately depressed head and body. Head width as broad as body. Dorsal body colour light grey or brown, with or without dark spots. Skin fold on posterior margin of thigh. Digits webbed at bases and broadly dilated. All digits have claws; first (inner) claw concealed. Males have 32–40 precloacal femoral pore-bearing scales. Juveniles have very small black and white spots. **DISTRIBUTION** Apo, Balicasag, Bantayan, Bohol, Bonoon, Boracay, Calagna-an, Caluya, Camiguin Sur, Carabao, Cebu, Clara, Danjugan, Duitay, Guimaras,

Inampulugan, Jao, Lapinig Chico, Lapinig Grande, Leyte, Luzon, Mactan, Mantique, Marinduque, Mindanao, Mindoro, Nadulao, Negros, Pacijan, Palawan, Panay, Panubolon, Pan de Azucar, Ponson, Poro, Samar, Sibuyan, Sicogon, Siquijor, Gigantes Sur, Tablas, Tilmubo. **HABITS AND HABITAT** Human commensal gecko. Feeds mainly on insects and arachnids, but also on flower nectar. Occurs from sea level to 600m asl. Females usually lay two eggs, which are adhered to wall crevices. **NOTE** The skin of this gecko is easily torn if handled improperly.

Hatchling

Adult

Palawan Gecko ■ *Gekko athymus* SVL 120mm

DESCRIPTION Dorsal colour dark greyish-brown with light and dark 'V'-shaped markings; 10–20 transverse tubercle rows at mid-body. Ventral pale yellow with scattered dark spots. Scansors beneath fourth toe: 16–22. Tail squarish in cross-section, without spines or tubercles,, dark brown with yellow bands. **DISTRIBUTION** Palawan. **HABITS AND HABITAT** Nocturnal and arboreal. Inhabits forests at 60–650m asl. Microhabits include leaf axils and loose bark on tree trunks. Females lay two eggs per clutch. Hatchlings 33.4–35.1mm SVL.

Luzon Karst Gecko ■ *Gekko carusadensis* SVL 97mm

DESCRIPTION Moderate-sized gecko. Dorsal body grey with no dark mottling or few transverse bars; 16–18 tubercles per row at mid-body. Can be distinguished from the Mindoro Narrow-disked Gekko (p. 43), the most morphologically similar species, as follows: male has 46–50 precloacofemoral pores arranged in uninterrupted series (v 52–66), and 18–20 scansors beneath fourth toe (v 12–14). Tail has transverse bars, darkest posteriorly. **DISTRIBUTION** Luzon. **HABITS AND HABITAT** Nocturnal. Inhabits karst outcrops and caves at low elevation. **NOTE** Recently described; very limited information available on its natural history.

Leonardo Co's Forest Gecko ■ *Gekko coi* SVL 84mm (e)

DESCRIPTION Dorsal medium brown to grey with light and dark brown blotches; 16–18 scansors beneath fourth toe; 13–15 transverse row of tubercles at mid-body. Males have 85–92 contiguous precloacofemoral pores. Alternating light and dark bands on tail. **DISTRIBUTION** Sibuyan. **HABITS AND HABITAT** Nocturnal and arboreal. Inhabits lowland forests in riparian habitats. Usually seen on tree trunks and boulders near the ground. **NOTE** Species named in honour of Leonardo Co, a respected Filipino botanist.

Ernst Keller's Gecko ■ *Gekko ernstkelleri* SVL 92mm (e)

DESCRIPTION Dorsal greyish-brown to dark olive with white and brown spots, especially on head and neck region; 11–15 transverse row of dorsal tubercles at mid-body. Ventral white with fine brown dots; 17–19 scansors beneath fourth toe. Males have 36–42 precloacal femoral pores. Tail slightly swollen at base and has narrow transverse white bands. **DISTRIBUTION** Panay. **HABITS AND HABITAT** Inhabits limestone caves in forests and rock outcrops on shores from sea level to 300m asl. Often seen near cave entrances and surrounding vegetation. Females lay two eggs per clutch. Eggs glued in crevices on cave roofs near entrances. Hatchlings 34.7–35.5mm SVL.

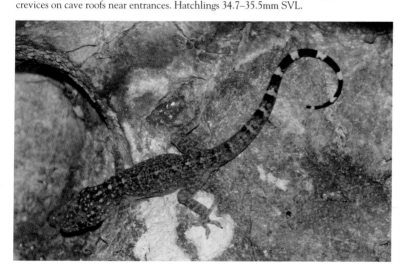

Hatchling

Adult

Tokay Gecko ■ *Gekko gecko gecko* SVL 155mm; TL 310mm

DESCRIPTION Large gecko with grey base colour on head, body, legs and tail. Head large and distinct from neck. Orange spots on head, body and limbs, fading on tail, often combined with eight transversely alligned rows of white spots. White spots often absent on head. Tail as long as SVL. Juveniles generally more bold in colouration than adults, and have transverse white bands on body and tail. **DISTRIBUTION** Apo, Bantayan, Bohol, Boracay, Busuanga, Calagna-an, Caluya, Camiguin Sur, Carabao, Cebu, Danjugan, Gigantes Norte, Guimaras, Inampulugan, Jolo, Lahuy, Lapinig Chico, Lapinig Grande, Leyte, Luzon, Mantique, Marinduque, Mindanao, Mindoro, Negros, Pacijan, Palawan, Pamilican, Panay, Pan de Azucar, Ponson, Poro, Semirara, Sibay, Sicogon, Siquijor, Sumilon, Tablas, Tilmubo. **HABITS AND HABITAT** Nocturnal and arboreal. Commonly seen in rural houses on walls and in secondary forests on tree trunks. Seen in both lowland and hill dipterocarp forests. Found hiding in rock cracks or under tree bark by day. Sometimes occurs up to 5m above the ground at night. Call, *to-kay*, repeated several times, and diagnostic for species. Feeds mainly on invertebrates (cockroaches, beetles, crickets), and opportunistically on vertebrates (geckos, small birds, house mice). Females lay two eggs that are adhered to insides of tree holes. Hatchlings about 40mm SVL.

Kikuchi's Gecko ■ *Gekko kikuchii* SVL 80mm

DESCRIPTION Dorsal uniform greyish-brown with paired dark spots from neck to tail-base. Upper labials: 13, lower labials: 10. Scattered white tubercles on dorsum, limbs and tail; 14 lamellae beneath fourth toe. Males have 24 femoral pores on each thigh. Tail tapering, slightly depressed and with transverse dark bands. **DISTRIBUTION** Luzon. **HABITS AND HABITAT** Nocturnal and arboreal. Common in limestone caves, where it can be seen near cave entrances, on walls and ceilings. Females lay two eggs per clutch, which are glued to walls or ceilings.

Mindoro Narrow-disked Gecko ■ *Gekko mindorensis* SVL 88mm ⓔ

DESCRIPTION Moderate-sized gecko with slightly depressed body. Dorsal body grey with thin, dark transverse bands. Tubercles at mid-body: 16–20 per row. Males have 52–66 precloacal femoral pores arranged in uninterrupted series, and 12–14 scansors beneath fourth toe. Adult female slightly smaller than male. **DISTRIBUTION** Caluya, Camiguin Sur, Catanduanes, Cebu, Cotivas, Guimaras, Luzon, Masbate, Mindoro, Negros, Panay, Panglao, Tanasac. **HABITS AND HABITAT** Occurs from sea level to 900m asl in and near entrances of limestone caves. Eggs usually glued to cave walls.

Palawan Narrow-disked Gecko ▪ *Gekko palawanensis* SVL 66mm ⓔ

DESCRIPTION Small gecko with grey or brown dorsal body and paired dark spots. Scales on head small and uniform in size; 64–70 precloacal femoral pore-bearing scales. No webbing between digits; 16–19 scansors beneath fourth toe. **DISTRIBUTION** Palawan. **HABITS AND HABITAT** Arboreal and nocturnal. Occurs from sea level to 900m asl. Usually seen close to the ground on tree trunks, beneath loose bark and on roofs of small caves.

Brooke's House Gecko ▪ *Hemidactylus brookii* SVL 56mm

DESCRIPTION Cryptic species with confused taxonomic history. Body light to dark brown, with or without dark spots. Ear opening large, oval and slanted. Upper labials: 8–10, lower labials: 9–11. Dorsal body has large tubercles forming 16–19 longitudinal rows. Two series of 12–13 precloacal femoral pores separated in middle by non-pore-bearing scale in male; 7–8 lamellae beneath fourth toe. Anterior portion of tail has recurved conical spines. Subcaudal scales longer than high and cover entire ventral surface of tail. **DISTRIBUTION** Luzon. **HABITS AND HABITAT** Arboreal, nocturnal and human commensal. Common in houses and other man-made structures. Usually seen at night on walls while hunting for insects attracted by artificial lights.

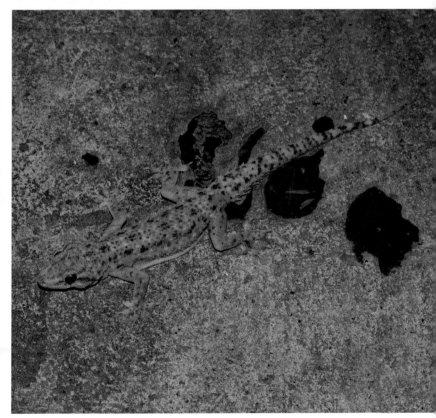

Common House Gecko ▪ *Hemidactylus frenatus* SVL 57mm; TL 114mm

DESCRIPTION Slender, with depressed body and head slightly distinct from neck. Dorsal body colour variable, from grey to light brown, with or without dark blotches or scattered small spots. Digits moderately dilated, with claws, and not webbed; 9–11 divided scansors beneath fourth toe. Tail slightly longer than SVL. Tail-sides have small, spiny scales at intervals of 7–12 scales; regenerated tail does not have spiny scales. **DISTRIBUTION** Agutayan, Apo, Balicasag, Bantayan, Basilan, Bohol, Bonoon, Boracay, Busuanga, Calagna-an, Caluya, Camiguin Sur, Carabao, Cataban, Cebu, Calotcot, Duitay, Gigantes Norte, Gigantes Sur, Great Govenen, Guimaras, Islet de Cresta de Gallo, Jao, Jolo, Lahuy, Lapinig Chico, Lapinig Grande, Leyte, Luzon, Mactan, Mindanao, Mindoro, Nadulao, Negros, Olango, Pacijan, Palawan, Pamilican, Pan De Azucar, Panay, Panubolon, Polong Dako, Ponson, Poro, Semirara, Sibay, Sibuyan, Sicogon, Siquijor, Sumilon, Tablas, Tintiman, Marinduque, Tilmubo. **HABITS AND HABITAT** Arboreal, nocturnal and human commensal. Very common in human settlements, even in urban areas. Often congregates near light fixtures to hunt insects attracted to light. Females lay pair of round, hard-shelled eggs. Incubation period 50–70 days. Hatchlings 19–22mm SVL; 37–42mm TL.

Flat-tailed House Gecko ■ *Hemidactylus platyurus* SVL 58mm; TL 120mm

DESCRIPTION Moderate-sized, with depressed body and tail. Head tapering and slightly distinct from neck; 9–12 upper labial scales, with 8th–10th beneath centre of eye. Body light grey or brown with spots and blotches. Prominent skin-fringes on sides of body and posterior edges of hindlimbs. Lamellae beneath fourth toe: 7–9. Tail very depressed, with marginal fringes. **DISTRIBUTION** Apo, Bohol, Cebu, Jolo, Leyte, Luzon, Marinduque, Mindanao, Negros, Panay, Sibuyan. **HABITS AND HABITAT** Mainly arboreal and nocturnal. Human commensal and common in urban and rural areas; hunts insects near artificial lights. Females lay pair of round, hard-shelled eggs. Hatchlings 20–25mm SVL.

Luzon

Palawan

Stejneger's House Gecko ■ *Hemidactylus stejnegeri* SVL 60mm; TL 120mm

DESCRIPTION Dorsum light greyish-brown with faint brown and white markings. Head depressed with rounded snout. Upper labials: 10–14. Dorsal body covered with very small, granular scales, without enlarged tubercles. Limbs have white spots. Scansors beneath fourth toe: 12–14. Tail depressed, with spots and serrated lateral edges. Can be

distinguished from the Common House Gecko (p. 46) by lack of enlarged tubercles on body and number of scansors beneath fourth toe; from the Flat-tailed House Gecko (p. 47) by lack of skin-fringes on lateral body and posterior of hindlimbs. **DISTRIBUTION** Cebu, Luzon, Mindanao, Mindoro, Panay. **HABITS AND HABITAT** Nocturnal and arboreal. Occurs in forests, but more commonly seen with other house geckos. Usually seen on walls and ceilings of structures, preying on invertebrates attracted by artificial light.

Philippine Slender Gecko ■ *Hemiphyllodactylus insularis*
SVL 37mm; TL 74mm

DESCRIPTION Small, inconspicuous gecko with egg-shaped head and slender body. Dorsum light brown to greyish-brown with irregular black markings. Row of small, reddish spots from behind eye to tail-base. Dorsal and ventral scalation granular. Upper and lower labials: 9–11. Ventral yellowish-brown with brown spots. Limbs relatively short. Digits have expanded pads and claws; 7–10 precloacal and 9–12 femoral pores in males, always separated. Females do not have pores. Cloacal spurs: 0–3. Tail light brown with scattered black spots; tail-tip cream. **DISTRIBUTION** Basilan, Bohol, Cebu, Leyte, Mindanao, Mindoro, Negros, Palawan, Panay. **HABITS AND HABITAT** Arboreal and nocturnal. Inhabits beaches, mangroves and lowland forests to 500m asl. Usually found beneath bark of trees. Females lay two light brown eggs per clutch, which are attached under tree bark.

Common Smooth-scaled Gecko ◾ *Lepidodactylus lugubris* SVL 45mm

DESCRIPTION All-female, parthenogenetic species. Males rarely seen, and are infertile. Dorsal body light brown to greyish-brown, with small dark spots and wavy lines. Pair of dark, round or oval spots behind neck. Rostral scale in contact with nostril. Scansors beneath fourth toe: 12–18. Tail has dark, narrow, wavy transverse bands, usually lighter in colour than body. **DISTRIBUTION** Apo, Agutayan, Balicasag, Basilan, Bonoon, Boracay, Calagna-an, Carabao, Cataban, Cebu, Clara, Gigantes Sur, Greater Govenen, Inampulugan, Jao, Lapinig Chico, Lapinig Grande, Little Govenen, Luzon, Mactan, Nadulao, Negros, Pacijan, Palawan, Pan de Azucar, Panay, Panubolon, Polong Dako, Ponson, Poro, Sicogon, Sumilon, Tintiman. **HABITS AND HABITAT** Arboreal, inhabiting mainly coastal habitats such as mangroves and beach forests. Usually seen on trees and bare rocks near shores. Female lays two eggs that are adhered between leaf axils. Hatchlings 16–18mm SVL.

Flat-tailed Smooth-scaled Gecko ■ *Lepidodactylus planicaudus*
SVL 42mm ⓔ

DESCRIPTION Dorsum brown to reddish-brown with broad, lighter brown mid-dorsal stripe. Head, body and tail depressed. Upper labials: 10–13. Limbs relatively short with dilated digits; 7–11 scansors beneath fourth toe. Ventral pale yellow to brown, with or without small dark spots; 18–25 precloacal femoral pores in males. Lateral of tail has broad skin-fringe and enlarged, spine-like scales. Subcaudal may be bright orange with

Adult

transverse black bands.
DISTRIBUTION Mindanao, Mindoro, Negros, Panay.
HABITS AND HABITAT Nocturnal and arboreal. Inhabits primary forests to agroforests at sea level to 700m asl. May display colourful subcaudal when disturbed or threatened. Females lay 1–2 eggs per clutch, which are adhered to leaf axil or beneath tree bark. Hatchlings 14.6–16.0mm SVL.

Hatchling

Bicol Smooth-scaled Gecko ■ *Lepidodactylus bisakol* SVL 39mm

DESCRIPTION Dorsum grey to light brown with light, 'V'-shaped (chevron) pattern. Rostral scale not in contact with nostril. Postocular white stripe; 9–11 scansors beneath fourth toe. Males have total of 23–27 precloacal femoral pores. Tail wide at base and round in cross-section. Sides of tail have enlarged scales resembling spikes. Closely resembles and occurs in sympantry with the Common Smooth-scaled Gecko (p. 49), but can be distinguished from it by fewer scansors beneath fourth toe (v 12–18), and rostral not in contact with nostril (v in contact). **DISTRIBUTION** Luzon (Bicol Peninsula). **HABITS AND HABITAT** Nocturnal and arboreal. Newly described species in 2021. Inhabits forests at 50–643m asl, but has also been seen in buildings.

Corfield's Gecko ■ *Luperosaurus corfieldi* SVL 95mm; TL 160mm ⓔ

DESCRIPTION Robust, forest-obligate gecko. Dorsum light grey to reddish-brown with light and dark markings. Upper labials: 14–16. Dorsal scales granular with a few dorsolateral tubercles. Wide skin-fringes on forelimbs and posteriors of hindlimbs. Digits webbed and dilated; 16–19 scansors beneath fourth toe. Ventral off-white to yellow. Males have 16 precloacal pores. Tail slender, prehensile and with light brown bars. **DISTRIBUTION** Negros, Panay. **HABITS AND HABITAT** Arborial and nocturnal. Inhabits primary and secondary forests at 400–700m asl. Rarely seen and may be canopy specialist. Females lay two eggs per clutch. Incubation is at least six weeks. Hatchlings 33–35mm SVL.

Adult

Hatchling

West Visayas False Gecko

■ *Pseudogekko atiorum* SVL 54mm; TL 114mm e

DESCRIPTION Moderate-sized false gecko.
Dorsum brown with small light spots. Snout
lighter colour. Upper labials: 15–17, lower
labials: 12–15. Limbs slender; 14–17 scansors
beneath fourth toe. Males have 13–15 precloacal
pores; femoral pores absent. Tail without bands.
DISTRIBUTION Negros, Siquijor. **HABITS
AND HABITAT** Arboreal and nocturnal.
Primarily forest obligate, but has been found
in agricultural areas within secondary forests.
No other information on ecology and biology
currently available.

Hatchling

Adult

Blue Eye-ringed False Gecko ■ *Pseudogekko compresicorpus*
SVL 60mm; TL 117mm ⓔ

DESCRIPTION Dorsum light grey to dark brown with light green spots. Diagnostic light blue eye-ring. Upper labials: 16–20, lower labials: 13–16. Ventral light grey with some brown mottling on lateral margins; 18–19 scansors beneath fourth toe. Males have 10–14 precloacal pores; femoral pores absent. Tail has cream blotches. **DISTRIBUTION** Luzon, Masbate, Polillo, Romblon, Tablas. **HABITS AND HABITAT** Arboreal and nocturnal. Inhabits forests and usually seen on small trees and vegetation 2–4m above the ground.

Southern Philippine False Gecko
■ *Pseudogekko pungkaypinit* SVL 77mm; TL 141mm ⓔ

DESCRIPTION Large, overall greyish-brown false gecko with series of light brown or yellow diagonal stripes on lateral body. Upper labials: 16–20, lower labials: 17–19. Scansors beneath fourth toe: 17–21; precloacal pores in males: 17–20. Tail same colour as dorsal body and with a few cream spots. **DISTRIBUTION** Bohol, Leyte, Mindanao. **HABITS AND HABITAT** Arboreal forest obligate. Usually seen on leaves of shrubs 2–4m above the ground.

Polillo False Gecko ▪ *Pseudogekko smaragdinus* SVL 64mm; TL 130mm

DESCRIPTION Slender, brightly coloured gecko. Dorsum bright yellow to yellow-orange (when undisturbed) to yellow-green (when disturbed). Head and body have round and oval dark spots and a few scattered smaller white spots. Scansors beneath fourth toe: 16–22; 32–41 enlarged precloacal pores in males. Tail brownish-orange with white bands. **DISTRIBUTION** Luzon, Polillo. **HABITS AND HABITAT** Arboreal forest obligate. Usually found between leaf axils of *Pandanus* trees.

Philippine Parachute Gecko ▪ *Gekko intermedium*
SVL 100mm; TL 189mm

DESCRIPTION Unusual gecko with characteristic skin-flaps on head, lateral body and limbs. Dorsum light grey to light reddish-brown with five thin, dark, wavy transverse bands from nape to tail-base. Dorsal body has irregular rows of tubercles; 8–12 pore-bearing precloacal scales; 12–19 pore-bearing (in males) and dimpled (in females) femoral scales. Extensive webbing between digits. Tail has scalloped lobes on lateral margins. Terminal skin-flap short and narrow (3.2–8.0mm). **DISTRIBUTION** Dinagat, Leyte, Mindanao, Maripipi. **HABITS AND HABITAT** Arboreal and nocturnal. Inhabits forests and agroforests. Most commonly seen on tree trunks and branches in agroforests. Employs escape behaviour by launching itself to the ground, and remaining motionless.

SCINCIDAE (SKINKS)
This is the most diverse lizard family, with more than 1,700 species. Most are terrestrial, while others are arboreal, semi-aquatic or fossorial. Typical skinks are diurnal and have smooth scales, moderate body size, and four limbs with five digits on each. Several semi-fossorial skinks have reduced limbs/digits or are limbless. Some species give birth to live young.

Bicol Loam Swimming Skink ■ *Brachymeles makusog*
SVL 124mm; TL 241mm (e)

DESCRIPTION Large skink with relatively short limbs and five digits. Dorsum light orange-brown with irregular brown streaks to tail-tip. Supranasals, prefrontals and parietals not in contact; fourth or fifth upper labial beneath centre of eye; pineal eye-spot present; 25–28 scale rows at mid-body. Can be distinguished from all other five-digit *Brachymeles* by having fully developed limbs and 8–9 lamellae beneath fourth toe, and lacking third pair of enlarged chin-shields. **DISTRIBUTION** Catanduanes, Luzon. **HABITS AND HABITAT** Fossorial and diurnal. Occurs in primary and secondary forests at 200–1,100m asl. Usually found under leaf litter and humus of rotting logs.

Masbate Slender Skink ■ *Brachymeles mapalanggaon*
SVL 76mm; TL 120mm (e)

DESCRIPTION Small skink with slender body and digitless limbs. Dorsum uniform brown. Upper labials: six, lower labials: 5–6. Scale rows at mid-body: 22–23. Pineal eye-spot may be present or absent; 2–3 pairs of enlarged chin-shields. **DISTRIBUTION** Masbate. **HABITS AND HABITAT** Fossorial and diurnal. Occurs in forests and found under rotting logs. Very limited information available on ecology and biology.

Palawan Tree Skink

■ *Dasia griffini* SVL 116mm; TL 224mm

DESCRIPTION Large *Dasia* with robust body and well-developed limbs. Dorsum brown with dark scales forming 8–10 transverse bands between axilla and tail-base. Dorsal scales have three keels; 26–28 scale rows at mid-body and 17–20 lamellae beneath fourth toe. Ventral pale green. **DISTRIBUTION** Palawan. **HABITS AND HABITAT** Arboreal and diurnal. Inhabits forests and disturbed areas up to 150m asl. Usually seen on trees by day.

Mangrove Skink ■ *Emoia atrocostata* SVL 8mm; TL 226mm

DESCRIPTION Elongated skink with greyish-olive dorsum that can be flecked with dark brownish or greyish. Ventral area bluish, greyish or cream, with dark markings on throat. **DISTRIBUTION** Babuyan, Bancoran, Bantayan, Basilan, Bogas, Bohol, Busuanga, Calauit, Caluya, Cebu, Dinagat, Gigante Sur, Great Govenen, Guimaras, Inampulungan, Lapinig Chico, Lahuy, Luzon, Masbate, Mindanao, Mindoro, Negros, Palawan, Pan de Azucar, Panay, Polillo, Ponson, Samar, Siargao, Tablas. **HABITS AND HABITAT** Diurnal; strongly associated with coastal regions, sandy or rocky beaches, and mangrove forests. Can be seen basking on rocks and trees by day. Uses hollow tree trunks for shelter at high tide.

Pacific Blue-tailed Skink
■ *Emoia caeruleocauda* SVL 65mm

DESCRIPTION Small, robust-looking skink with dark base colour. Very bright, light blue tail and three golden stripes that radiate from just above eye (two stripes) or tip of snout (one), over dorsum towards tail, slowly changing colour to blue. Fading black, stripe-like markings on tail. **DISTRIBUTION** Comiran, Mindanao, Palawan, Tulian Rock (west of Jolo). **HABITS AND HABITAT** Diurnal and terrestrial. Occurs in wide range of habitats, including forest clearings, sandy beaches and rural gardens. In the Philippines seems to be associated with small, rocky islands.

Red-tailed Skink ■ *Emoia ruficauda* SVL 54mm

DESCRIPTION Part of *Emoia cyanura* species group (that is, in which nasal bones not fused) and *E. caeruleocauda* subgroup (rounded or moderately thinned subdigital lamellae). Easily identified by thinned subdigital lamellae (55–63) and colour pattern. Five yellow lines from tip of snout to tail-base. Dorsum body black; tail and limbs bright red/orange. **DISTRIBUTION** Mindanao. **HABITS AND HABITAT** Little known diurnal species. Can be relatively common in areas where it occurs. Previously found in disturbed and undisturbed primary lowland forests at 200–300m asl. Also in tall grass near lakes or rivers, on broad leaves on low shrubs, and on forest floor.

Caraga Sun Skink

■ *Eutropis caraga* SVL 84mm

DESCRIPTION Medium-sized skink with iridescent brown to olive dorsum. Lateral head and body dark brown with faint brown stripes above and below. Parietals separated by interparietal scale. Dorsal scales have 5–10 keels; 80–90 total lamellae beneath all toes on one foot. Dorsal limbs medium to dark brown with white spots. **DISTRIBUTION** Dinagat, Leyte, Mindanao, Samar, Siargao. **HABITS AND HABITAT** Diurnal and terrestrial. Found among leaf litter on forest floors and disturbed areas at sea level to 1,500m asl.

Luzon Sun Skink ■ *Eutropis cumingi* SVL 60mm

DESCRIPTION Small skink with brown to dark brown dorsum. Prominent, narrow cream dorsolateral stripe from snout to hindlimb. Second narrow cream stripe starts from upper labials and may extend to hindlimb insertion. Lower labials and sides of neck reddish-orange. Dorsal scales have 5–10 keels; 26–33 scale rows at mid-body. Limbs dark brown. Total lamellae beneath all toes on one foot: 59–70. Ventral greyish-cream. **DISTRIBUTION** Batan, Camiguin Norte, Luzon, Sabtang. **HABITS AND HABITAT** Diurnal and terrestrial. Inhabits primary and secondary forests. Usually seen on the ground basking by day.

Palawan Sun Skink ■ *Eutropis sahulinghangganan* SVL 63mm ⓔ

DESCRIPTION Small skink with prominent bright orange marking on ventral side of head and neck. Dorsum iridescent bronze to olive, with extensive dark brown flecks. Pair of narrow cream dorsolateral stripes may be irregularly bordered with black scales. Dorsal scales have 5–10 keels; 28–33 scale rows at mid-body; 63–77 total lamellae beneath all toes on one foot. Tail olive to reddish-brown. **DISTRIBUTION** Palawan. **HABITS AND HABITAT** Diurnal and terrestrial. Occurs in forests and disturbed areas from sea level to 1,500m asl.

Many-lined Sun Skink ■ *Eutropis multifasciata* SVL 130mm; TL 351mm

DESCRIPTION Highly variable, robust-looking skink with short snout. Dorsum generally bronze or brown. Male has bright yellow, orange or reddish flanks during breeding

season. There may be five or seven dark lines on dorsum. Three keels on dorsal scales. **DISTRIBUTION** Widespread, including Luzon, Mindanao, Panay. **HABITS AND HABITAT** Very common diurnal species. Often seen basking in the sun along forest trails, on the ground, or on tops of boulders and logs. Found in forest edges, grassland and urban gardens. Females give birth to 2–10 young per clutch. Hatchlings 36–43mm SVL.

Negros Forest Skink ■ *Insulasaurus arborens* SVL 66mm; TL 145mm ⓔ

DESCRIPTION Dorsum light brown to reddish-brown with row of median black spots. Snout short and bluntly rounded; 36–39 scale rows at mid-body. Black dorsolateral stripe starting from snout becomes irregular spots and continues on tail; 18–22 lamellae beneath fourth toe. **DISTRIBUTION** Masbate, Negros, Panay, Pan de Azucar. **HABITS AND HABITAT** Diurnal and arboreal. Occurs in primary and secondary forests, and agricultural areas adjacent to forests. Commonly seen along stream banks or resting on shrubs.

Adult

Hatchling

Philippine Emerald Tree Skink

■ *Lamprolepis smaragdina philippinica*
SVL 107mm; TL 268mm e

DESCRIPTION Moderate-sized skink with various morphs such as bright green, green with black blotches on body, and green anteriorly and brown posteriorly. Head pointed; tail almost twice as long as body; scales smooth. DISTRIBUTION Basilan, Bohol, Bonoon, Boracay, Calicoan, Caluya, Camiguin Sur, Cebu, Greater Govenen, Inampulugan, Jao, Leyte, Luzon, Mindanao, Negros, Pacijan, Panay, Palawan, Siquijor, Siargao, Suluan. HABITS AND HABITAT Conspicuous arboreal skink commonly seen on tree trunks in gardens and other disturbed areas. Often seen in head-down position by day as it actively forages for insects. Also feeds on flower nectar. Oviparous; females lay two eggs per clutch in tree holes.

Yellow-striped Slender Tree Skink

■ *Lipinia pulchella pulchella* SVL 50mm; TL 125mm e

DESCRIPTION Slender skink with strongly depressed, tapered and pointed snout. Dorsum has yellow mid-dorsal stripe starting from snout, to tip of tail, bordered by dark brown stripes to tail-base. Limbs light brown with dark brown flecks. DISTRIBUTION Bohol, Dinagat, Leyte, Luzon, Mindanao, Polillo, Samar. HABITS AND HABITAT Diurnal and arboreal. Occurs in primary and secondary forests at 250–1,100m asl. Usually seen on tree trunks from near the ground to 3m high. Females lay 1–2 eggs per clutch, measuring 10.5mm in length. Hatchlings 21.1mm SVL.

Four-striped Slender Tree Skink ▪ *Lipinia quadrivittata* SVL 41mm

DESCRIPTION Dorsum pale yellow or pale brownish-orange, with four dark brown stripes. Snout short and not strongly depressed; 18–20 scale rows at mid-body. Tail orange-brown or yellow-brown. **DISTRIBUTION** Bohol, Camiguin Sur, Cebu, Dinagat, Leyte, Little Govenen, Mindanao, Negros, Palawan, Samar, Siquijor, Unib. **HABITS AND HABITAT** Diurnal and arboreal. Occurs in forests at sea level to 800m asl. Hides in aerial ferns, leaf axils of palm trees and crevices of tree trunks. Probably a species complex due to its disjunct distribution.

Rabor's Slender Tree Skink ▪ *Lipinia rabori* SVL 55mm; TL 121mm (e)

DESCRIPTION Dorsum dark brown with three prominent, golden-yellow stripes. Snout depressed and tapering. Throat has pale pink spots; 22 scale rows at mid-body. Limbs brown with irregular dark brown spots; 18–21 lamellae beneath fourth toe. Tail greenish-blue. Subcaudal blue. **DISTRIBUTION** Negros, Panay. **HABITS AND HABITAT** Diurnal and arboreal. Occurs in dipterocarp and submontane forests at 300–1,100m asl. Active by day on tree trunks.

Vulcan Slender Tree Skink
■ *Lipinia vulcania* SVL 50mm ⓔ

DESCRIPTION Dorsum reddish-brown with small, dark brown spots. Snout short and blunt. Broad, dark brown dorsolateral stripe from behind eye to hindlimb insertion; 30–32 scale rows at mid-body. Tail brownish-orange. **DISTRIBUTION** Mindanao (Zamboanga). **HABITS AND HABITAT** Diurnal and arboreal. Occurs in forests and often seen on tree trunks.

Palawan Supple Skink ■ *Lygosoma tabonorum* SVL 79mm; TL 151mm ⓔ

DESCRIPTION Small supple skink with relatively long body and short limbs. Dorsum uniform light brown with darker brown speckling. Upper and lower labials have brown spots. Tail shorter than SVL. **DISTRIBUTION** Cuyo, Palawan. **HABITS AND HABITAT** Diurnal and terrestrial. Occurs in primary and secondary forests. Active in the open by day, and mostly seen in decaying log microhabitats.

Philippine Giant Forest Skink ■ *Otosaurus cumingi*
SVL 135mm; TL 333mm ⓔ

DESCRIPTION Large, robust skink;
the only forest skink in the region
with large supranasal scales and
larger body than other related skinks.
Dorsum and head brownish with black
markings, resulting in incomplete
transverse bands. Black band from eye
towards tail, frequently interrupted
by yellowish spots, sometimes so
close together that they form vertical
bands. Ventral area greyish or
creamish. Legs have marbled pattern.
DISTRIBUTION Luzon, Mindanao.
HABITS AND HABITAT Often seen
on rocks or logs by day, or foraging
under leaves and logs. Occurs at
200–500m asl.

Mt Makiling Dwarf Skink ■ *Parvoscincus abstrusus* SVL 45mm ⓔ

DESCRIPTION Body small and slender. Dorsum brown with dark brown vertebral spots
from head to tail. Head black and throat black with small bluish spots (males); head
reddish-brown and throat cream (females). Two anterior loreals. Upper labials: six; lower
labials: seven. Dorsal scales have weak or no apical pits; 33–38 scale rows at mid-body;
15–19 lamellae beneath fourth toe. **DISTRIBUTION** Luzon, Polillo. **HABITS AND
HABITAT** Occurs in primary and secondary forests at 450–800m asl. Usually seen in leaf
litter and under logs.

Mt Palali Dwarf Skink ■ *Parvoscincus palaliensis* SVL 39mm

DESCRIPTION Dorsum brown with series of small, dark vertebral spots from neck region to tail-base. Seven upper and lower labials. Single anterior loreal. Dorsal scales without apical pits. Lateral body brown with white spots; 32 scale rows at mid-body; 14 lamellae beneath fourth toe. **DISTRIBUTION** Luzon. **HABITS AND HABITAT** Currently only known to occur in montane forests at 1,374–1,450m asl. Seen in leaf litter and near rotting logs.

Sison's Dwarf Skink ■ *Parvoscincus sisoni* SVL 37mm

DESCRIPTION Very small skink with slender body and medium brown dorsum. Six upper and lower labials. Dorsal scales smooth; 24–26 scale rows at mid-body; 11-12 lamellae beneath fourth toe. Ventral at mid-body has medium brown blotches. Subcaudal uniform brown. **DISTRIBUTION** Panay. **HABITS AND HABITAT** Occurs in montane forests at 900–1,600m asl. Seen in leaf litter of forest floors.

Northern Philippine Giant Forest Skink

■ *Pinoyscincus abdictus aquilonius* SVL 96mm ⓔ

DESCRIPTION Large skink with light to dark brown dorsum and broad black dorsolateral stripe interrupted into blotches or bands anteriorly. Snout moderately tapered and rounded at tip. Four large supraoculars (v five on nominate form). Anterior loreal single, higher than wide. Upper labials: 7–8, lower labials: seven. Scale rows at mid-body: 32–38; 62–73 scales from parietals to tail-base; 20–25 lamellae beneath fourth toe. **DISTRIBUTION** Babuyan Claro, Camiguin Norte, Calayan, Catanduanes, Dalupiri, Fuga, Lubang, Luzon, Polillo. **HABITS AND HABITAT** Diurnal and terrestrial. Occurs in primary and secondary forests. Often seen on leaf litter, riverbanks or tree buttresses while basking.

Jagor's Forest Skink ■ *Pinoyscincus jagori jagori* SVL 110mm ⓔ

DESCRIPTION Robust skink with well-developed limbs. Dorsum mottled brown to dark brown, with irregular narrow, light brown transverse bands. Snout moderately tapered and broadly rounded at tip. Two prominent dark bars, one beneath eye and another on posterior labials. Upper labials: six, lower labials: 6–8. Scale rows at mid-body: 36–42; 63–73 scales from parietals to tail-base; 24–30 lamellae beneath fourth toe. Tail blackish-brown. **DISTRIBUTION** Basilan, Bohol, Camiguin Sur, Dinagat, Leyte, Mindanao, Samar, Siargao. **HABITS AND HABITAT** Diurnal and terrestrial. Oviparous. Occurs in forests at near sea level to 600m asl. Commonly seen on forest leaf litter and under rotting logs. Females lay unknown number of eggs in forest floor. Hatchlings 28–33mm SVL.

Pointed-snouted Forest Skink ■ *Sphenomorphus acutus* SVL 76mm

DESCRIPTION Moderate-sized skink with slender body and pointed snout. Dorsum brown with series of light brown spots dorsolaterally. Black stripe from snout to behind eye, turning to irregular markings on anterior of forelimbs. Two anterior loreal scales; 26–30 scale rows at mid-body; 51–61 scales between parietals and tail-base; 28–36 lamellae beneath fourth toe. Tail long and brown with scattered black dots. Phylogenetic affinity of species uncertain. **DISTRIBUTION** Bohol, Dinagat, Leyte, Mindanao, Samar. **HABITS AND HABITAT** Diurnal and arboreal. Occurs in primary forests and usually seen on arboreal subtrates (understorey twigs and branches), forest floor and stream banks. Seen sleeping at night in dried broad leaves hanging 1–2m above the ground.

Banded Forest Skink ■ *Sphenomorphus fasciatus* SVL 81mm ⓔ

DESCRIPTION Body long and slender, with tail longer than body. Dark brown base colour on dorsum; body covered in spots so closely placed together on dorsum that they form transverse bands. Spots yellowish or brownish on head and dorsal area, but whitish on flanks and tail. **DISTRIBUTION** Basilan, Bohol, Camiguin Sur, Leyte, Mantique, Mindanao, Samar. **HABITS AND HABITAT** Diurnal. Found under leaves and rotten logs, and between tree buttresses in dipterocarp and submontane forests. Common in low-elevation, disturbed second growth and coastal forests. Also found in overhangs of cliffs. Occurs from sea level to 1,200m asl.

Philippine Keeled Water Skink ■ *Tropidophorus grayi*
SVL 119mm; TL 232mm

DESCRIPTION Primarily characterized by spinose dorsal body scales. Dorsum base greyish-black, but may vary from brown to black. Ventral surface white and can have brown blotches. May have several lighter brown lateral stripes from back of neck to tail-tip. **DISTRIBUTION** Catanduanes, Cebu, Leyte, Luzon, Polillo, Masbate, Negros, Panay, Polillo, Samar. **HABITS AND HABITAT** Diurnal; secretive in habits, hiding in the water when threatened. Semi-aquatic, foraging in leaf litter along streams or in shallow water. Found mainly in crevices in clay or rocky banks along streams, but also under moist humus and logs on the forest floor or near forest streams to 800m asl. Appears abundant, and also found in secondary forests and (human) disturbed areas.

Misamis Keeled Water Skink ▪ *Tropidophorus misaminius*
SVL 112mm; TL 219mm (e)

DESCRIPTION Large, slender skink with strongly keeled dorsal scales. Dorsum brown with traces of blackish postocular streak. Cluster of white spots on temples, with a few

additional scattered white spots on neck. Ventral area whitish; throat, neck, palms, soles and posterior two-thirds of tail blackish. **DISTRIBUTION** Basilan, Camiguin Sur, Mindanao. **HABITS AND HABITAT** Semi-aquatic. Usually occurs near or in rocky beds and on stream banks. Occasionally found under rotten logs or on banks of cave streams.

Adult with regenerated tail

Partello's Keeled Water Skink ■ *Tropidophorus partelloi*

SVL 127mm; TL 212mm ⓔ

DESCRIPTION Relatively large skink with moderately tapered snout. Dorsum dark to dusky brown, with head usually slightly lighter; 7–9 irregular, narrow and light brown bands of 1–2 scale rows on dorsum. Ventral area cream, grey or yellowish. Both dorsal and lateral scales have low keels, with scales on tail raised to sharp spines posteriorly. **DISTRIBUTION** Dinagat, Mindanao. **HABITS AND HABITAT** Semi-aquatic. Ovoviviparous. Found in damp soil under logs or rocks in forested habitats at 450–1,200m asl.

Mt Busa, Sarangani

Bukidnon

> ### VARANIDAE (MONITOR LIZARDS)
> Members of the monitor lizard family are some of the largest extant reptiles in the world. They have long, forked tongues, flicked regularly to sense the air. The only three known frugivorous monitor lizards are all forest obligate and endemic to the Philippines.

Northern Luzon Forest Monitor Lizard

▪ *Varanus bitatawa* SVL 766mm; TL 1,800m **ⓔ**

DESCRIPTION Large-bodied monitor; black base colour with yellowish-green dots and spots. At least four rows of ocelli on body; head robust; nostril opening a slanted slit; well-developed, muscular limbs with curved claws. Tail has alternating broad, black and yellowish-green bands. One of three members of subgenus *Philippinosaurus*, a clade of the only known frugivorous monitor lizards in the world. **DISTRIBUTION** Luzon. **HABITS AND HABITAT** Highly secretive, arboreal and forest obligate. Diet includes fruits of *Pandanus*, *Canarium* and *Ficus*, and invertebrates such as land snails and hermit crabs. Most active in late morning to early afternoon. Telemetry study showed males with greater activity areas ($23km^2$) than females ($5.2km^2$). Oviparous; no other data currently known about reproductive biology.

Panay Forest Monitor Lizard ■ *Varanus mabitang*
SVL 700mm; TL 1,750mm

DESCRIPTION Large monitor with slender body and black dorsum. Head narrow, tapering and with prominent bulges above temporal region. Nostril slit-like and diagonally oriented. Limbs long and slender. Digits have strongly recurved claws. Ventral dark grey to black. Tail laterally compressed and prehensile. **DISTRIBUTION** Panay. **HABITS AND HABITAT** Diurnal and arboreal. Occurs in primary forests at sea level to 1,000m asl. Rarely seen in forest edges. Feeds on various forest fruits, and invertebrates such as crabs, snails and insects.

Southern Luzon Forest Monitor Lizard

■ *Varanus olivaceus* SVL 730mm; TL 1,760m ⓔ

DESCRIPTION First known member of subgenus *Philippinosaurus*, scientifically described in 1857. Large-bodied, forest-obligate lizard; greenish-grey with dark transverse bands on neck and dorsal body. Nostrils slit shaped. Scales around nostrils, eyes and labials may be bright yellow. Limbs usually darker than rest of body. Legs muscular with strongly curved claws, suitable for climbing and digging. Tail has 11–12 dark bands. **DISTRIBUTION** Catanduanes, Luzon, Polillo. **HABITS AND HABITAT** Diurnal, arboreal and secretive. Feeds on fruits and invertebrates such as insects, crustaceans and snails. Females lay 4–16 eggs per clutch. Average hatchling 160mm SVL; 410mm TL. Needs intact forests to thrive.

Bangon Water Monitor Lizard ■ *Varanus bangonorum*
SVL 390cm; TL 600cm ⓔ

DESCRIPTION Moderate-sized, slender monitor. Dorsum dark grey to black with up to six transverse rows of yellow spots or ocelli. Nuchal scales distinctly larger than head scales. Throat pale yellow with dark markings. Limbs have scattered yellow dots and spots. Tail triangular in cross-section, with transverse rows of oblong yellow spots. **DISTRIBUTION** Mindoro, Semirara. **HABITS AND HABITAT** Diurnal and terrestrial. Juveniles more arboreal than adults. Occurs in forests, forest edges and disturbed areas. Feeds on invertebrates, vertebrates and carrion.

Hatchling

Juvenile

Mindanao Water Monitor Lizard

■ *Varanus cumingi* SVL 600mm; TL 1,500mm ⓔ

DESCRIPTION Large monitor with muscular limbs. Overall black and yellow; black temporal stripe. Nostrils oval, near snout-tip. Amount of yellow on head and body variable; transverse rows and spots may fade with age. Mid-body scales: 120–150.
DISTRIBUTION Basilan, Mindanao, Samal, Siargao. **HABITS AND HABITAT** Terrestrial and diurnal. Young individuals feed mainly on insects; adults on fish, crabs, molluscs and carrion. Predators include birds of prey and the King Cobra (p. 157). Often seen in disturbed areas such as farmland and forest edges.

Enteng's Water Monitor Lizard
■ *Varanus dalubhasa* SVL 505mm; TL 1,106mm

DESCRIPTION Superficially similar to the Luzon Marbled Water Monitor Lizard (p. 80), but genetically more similar to the Western Visayas Water Monitor Lizard (p. 81). Dorsum predominantly dark grey to black with yellow dots and transverse row of yellow ocelli. Head elongated and tapering. Nostril round or oblong, closer to snout than eye. Narrower off-white or pale yellow stripe below black postocular stripe. Ventral off-white to pale yellow. Limbs have bright yellow spots and dots. Tail laterally compressed, triangular in cross-section, with transverse rows of oblong yellow spots. Mid-body scales: 138. **DISTRIBUTION** Catanduanes, Lahuy, Luzon, Polillo. **HABITS AND HABITAT** Diurnal and terrestrial. Occurs in forests, forest edges and agricultural areas. Feeds mainly on vertebrates and carrion.

Luzon Marbled Water Monitor Lizard

■ *Varanus marmoratus* SVL 450mm; TL 1,800mm (e)

DESCRIPTION Member of *V. salvator* complex. Black base colour and yellow spots on body and limbs. Snout has alternating light cream and black cross-bands; nostril round near snout-tip; light cream temporal streak between eye and ear opening (tympanum); nuchal scales enlarged. Juveniles have 4–6 transverse rows of large ocelli on body, limbs and tail that may vanish with age. Mid-body scales: 115–145. **DISTRIBUTION** Batan, Calayan, Lubang, Luzon. **HABITS AND HABITAT** Generalist, feeding on live vertebrates and invertebrates and their carcasses. Documented feeding on invasive, poisonous Marine Toad *Rhinella marina* with no apparent ill effects. Occasionally considered a pest due to habit of preying on domesticated animals such as chickens and ducks. Oviparous, laying 8–14 eggs per clutch. Typically found in various lowland habitats such as forests, mangroves, coasts, fishponds, farms and coconut groves.

Western Visayas Water Monitor Lizard

■ *Varanus nuchalis* SVL 550mm; TL 1,390mm (e)

DESCRIPTION Moderate-sized monitor with two distinct morphs: one overall black with or without bright yellow scales on limbs and tail, the other black with varying amount of white on head, and white or yellow oval spots. Nuchal scales very enlarged. Both morphs have thin mid- dorsal line and black temporal stripe. Mid-body scales: 136–169. **DISTRIBUTION** Apo, Cebu, Masbate, Negros, Panay, Sibuyan, Tablas, Ticao. **HABITS AND HABITAT** Active by day. Opportunistically feeds on invertebrates (insects, crustaceans), vertebrates (birds, rodents, frogs), and carrion. Documented feeding on invasive, poisonous Marine Toad without ill effects. Most common in lowland forests. Often seen in mangroves, fishponds, rice fields and other disturbed areas.

Palawan Water Monitor Lizard ■ *Varanus palawanensis*
SVL 790mm; TL 2,000mm ⓔ

DESCRIPTION Large monitor with robust body and limbs. Head, dorsal body and tail dark grey to black, with or without yellow spots. Nostrils round to oblong near snout-tip. Throat off-white or pale yellow with dark marbling. Ventral body off-white to yellowish. **DISTRIBUTION** Balabac, Busuanga, Calauit, Candaraman, Coron, Lagen, Malapina, Miniloc, Palawan, Sibutu. **HABITS AND HABITAT** Feeds on small vertebrates, invertebrates and carrion. Inhabits various ecosystems, such as lowland forests, mangroves, beaches and disturbed habitats.

Rasmussen's Water Monitor Lizard ■ *Varanus rasmusseni*
SVL 470mm; TL 1,220mm ⓔ

DESCRIPTION Moderate-sized monitor with dark brown to black dorsum. Nostril oval, closer to snout than eye. Ventral pale yellow. Throat has black spots and abdomen has dark cross-bars. Juveniles have 12 transverse rows of yellow spots. **DISTRIBUTION** Bitinan, Jolo, Tawi-Tawi. **HABITS AND HABITAT** Diurnal and terrestrial. Feeds on small animals and carrion. Juveniles often seen basking or resting on horizontal branches.

Samar Water Monitor Lizard ■ *Varanus samarensis*
SVL 530mm; TL 1,400mm ⓔ

DESCRIPTION Dorsum predominantly black with 5–6 transverse yellow bands (adults) or distinct ocelli (juveniles). Dorsal of head has irregular yellow markings. Black postocular stripe. Throat yellow, with or without dark spots. Limbs have scattered yellow spots. Ventral yellow with 9–15 cross-bars or bars on each side. **DISTRIBUTION** Bohol, Calicoan, Leyte, Samar. **HABITS AND HABITAT** Diurnal and terrestrial. Commonly seen in forest edges and disturbed areas, where it feeds on small animals and carrion.

Marine File Snake ▪ *Acrochordus granulatus* SVL 900mm; TL 1,000mm

DESCRIPTION Aquatic snake with small head and eyes. Dorsum dark grey with transverse light grey bars that usually do not join dorsally. Skin rather loose and covered with pointed granular scales. Tail tapering and short. **DISTRIBUTION** Bantayan, Calauit, Cebu, Guimaras, Luzon, Masbate, Negros, Palawan, Panay, Siquijor. **HABITS AND HABITAT** Aquatic and diurnal. Prefers shallow waters on sea coasts and freshwater rivers near coasts, but can dive 20m deep. Feeds mainly on gobies. Females can give birth to 10 live young per clutch.

> ### COLUBRIDAE (COLUBRIDS)
> This is the most diverse snake family, with more than 2,000 species due to the historical use of it as a repository of snake species that do not clearly belong to other families. Phylogenetical studies are slowly unravelling the affinities of genera in the family.

Philippine Paradise Tree Snake

▪ *Chrysopelea paradisi variabilis* SVL 770mm; TL 1,100mm Ⓔ

DESCRIPTION Long, slender snake with cylindrical body. Head distinct from neck; eyes large with round pupils. Dorsum uniform brown with or without red and black markings. One preocular, two postoculars and one loreal (sometimes absent or fused with prefrontal). Upper labials: nine, fourth to sixth in contact with eye, lower labials: 9–11. Dorsal scales smooth with apical pits; 17 scale rows at mid-body; 204–234 ventrals, last one divided; 116–154 paired subcaudals. Tail tapering and long. Dorsum of hatchlings and juveniles dark brown to black, with white or reddish-orange transverse bands. **DISTRIBUTION** Apuao, Balabac, Bantayan, Banton, Basilan, Bongao, Bubuan, Calayan, Camiguin, Cebu, Cotivas, Dalupiri, Dinagat, Jolo, Kalotkot, Leyte, Luzon (Prov.: Bataan, Batangas, Bulacan, Cavite, Laguna, Quezon, Rizal, Sorsogon, Zambales), Marongas, Masbate, Medis, Mindanao (Agusan del Norte, Zamboanga del Sur, Zamboanga City), Mindoro, Negros, Palawan, Panay (Aklan, Antique, Iloilo), Polillo, Romblon, Samar, Sanga_Sanga, Siagao, Sibuyan, Siquijor, Tablas, Tawi-Tawi, Unib (Dinagat Prov). **HABITS AND HABITAT** Arboreal and diurnal. Inhabits primary forests to disturbed areas from sea level to 1,000m asl. Feeds mainly on geckos and skinks such as *Cyrtodactylus* spp., Tokay Gecko (p. 42) and Philippine Emerald Tree Skink (p. 62). Well known for ablity to glide from canopy to lower branches of trees.

Hatchling

Adult

Asian Vine Snake ▪ *Ahaetulla prasina prasina* SVL 930mm; TL 1,440mm

DESCRIPTION Long, slender snake with narrow, elongated head. Deep depression from eye to snout. Pupil horizontal. One preocular and two postoculars; upper larger. Dorsum yellowish-green. Dorsal head and upper labials have scattered grey dots. Interstitial skin on anterior third of body has short, black and white, slanted streaks when body is distended. Upper labials: nine, fourth to sixth in contact with eye, lower labials: 8–9. Precloacal scale divided. Tail slender and long. **DISTRIBUTION** Balabac, Busuanga, Calauit, Coron, Culion, Palawan. **HABITS AND HABITAT** Diurnal and arboreal. Occurs in forests and often seen in branches of shrubs and small trees. Predates on small geckos and skinks. Females give birth to 1–11 young.

Philippine Vine Snake ■ *Ahaetulla prasina preocularis*
SVL 1,000mm; TL 1,700mm ⓔ

DESCRIPTION Typical form uniform green, but other morphs such as yellow, reddish-brown, blue and white also occur. Head elongated, with large eye and horizontal pupil, and no markings. Two or more preocular scales. Upper labials: nine, fourth to sixth in contact with eye, lower labials: seven. Precloacal scale not divided. Tail slender and long, about 34–40 per cent of TL.

Brown

DISTRIBUTION Basilan, Batan, Bohol, Camiguin Norte, Camiguin Sur, Cebu, Dinagat, Jolo, Leyte, Luzon, Marinduque, Masbate, Mindanao, Mindoro, Negros, Panay, Polillo, Sabtang, Samar, Sibutu, Tablas. **HABITS AND HABITAT** Diurnal and arboreal. Occurs in forests and coconut groves from sea level to 1,200m asl. Often seen motionless on branches of shrubs and small trees. Predates on small geckos, skinks and frogs. Females give birth to 4–7 live young per clutch.

Yellow

Blue

Green

White

Sulu Vine Snake ■ *Ahaetulla prasina suluensis* SVL 1,000mm; TL 1,500mm

DESCRIPTION Yellowish-green, slender snake with elongated head. Eyes large with horizontal pupil. One preocular and two postoculars, upper larger. Upper labials: nine, lower labials: 8–9. Loreal scale in contact with nasal very small. Precloacal scale divided. Tail slender and very long. **DISTRIBUTION** Bongao, Sanga-Sanga, Siasi, Sibutu, Tawi-Tawi. **HABITS AND HABITAT** Diurnal and arboreal. Occurs in forests and often seen on branches of shrubs and small trees. Ovoviviparous.

Leviton's Bronzeback Snake
■ *Dendrelaphis levitoni* SVL 980mm; TL 1,310mm

DESCRIPTION Long, slender snake with brown dorsum. Head distinct from neck, with 4–6 temporal scales. Eyes large with round pupils. Upper labials: nine, lower labials: 9–11. Postocular stripe extends to neck and merges with longitudinal stripe on body. Bright reddish-orange on neck extends on body and gradually fades posteriorly. Black ventrolateral line. Dorsal scales smooth; 13 scale rows at mid-body. Ventrals: 175–181 (males) to 180–189 (females); subcaudals: 101–116. Anal plate divided. Tail length 25–28 per cent of TL. **DISTRIBUTION** Balabac, Candaraman, Miniloc, North Guntao, Palawan. **HABITS AND HABITAT** Diurnal and mainly arboreal. Feeds on geckos and frogs. An individual was documented being predated by a King Cobra (p. 157) on North Guntao Island.

Luzon Bronzeback Snake ■ *Dendrelaphis luzonensis*
SVL 980mm; TL 1,300mm

DESCRIPTION Dorsum light to medium brown. Head distinct from neck, with 5–7 temporal scales. Eyes large with round pupils. Upper labials: nine, lower labials: 9–11. Postocular stripe present or absent; 6–8 black longitudinal stripes; black ventrolateral stripe on posterior half of body. Dorsal scales smooth; 13 scale rows at mid-body. Ventral pale yellowish-green. Ventrals 176–182 (males) to subcaudals 178–187 (females) and 100–117. Anal plate divided. Tail length 25–29 per cent of TL. **DISTRIBUTION** Calayan, Camiguin Norte, Catonavan, Dalupiri, Luzon, Marinduque, Sabitang-Laya. **HABITS AND HABITAT** Diurnal and mainly arboreal. Inhabits forests from sea level to 800m asl. Commonly seen on trees along banks of forest streams and rivers. Feeds on geckos, skinks *Eutropis* spp. and frogs.

Maren's Bronzeback Snake ■ *Dendrelaphis marenae*
SVL 858 mm; TL 1,300mm

DESCRIPTION Bronze-coloured, long, slender snake. Enlarged vertebral scales distinguish it from rest of *Dendrelaphis* spp. in the Philippines. Head elongated and slightly distinct from neck. Eyes large with round pupils. One preocular, two postoculars, nine loreals. Upper labials: nine, fourth to sixth in contact with eye, lower labials: 10. Broad postocular black stripe extends to body; gradually fades posteriorly. Short blue bars along black stripe appear when body is distended. Ventrals light greenish-yellow. **DISTRIBUTION** Balabac, Bantayan, Basilan, Bohol, Bongao, Busuanga, Calauit, Camiguin, Candaraman, Carabao, Catanduanes, Catonavan, Cebu, Culion, Guimaras, Jolo, Kalotkot, Lagen, Leyte, Luzon, Mapun, Marinduque, Masbate, Mindanao, Mindoro, Negros, Palawan, Panay, Polillo, Samar, Siargao, Siquijor, Surigao, Tablas. **HABITS AND HABITAT** Agile snake that actively hunts frogs and toads, including the Philippine Toad *Ingerophyrus philippinicus*, on the ground, and geckos on trees by day. Occurs in riparian habitats, forest edges, agricultural areas and gardens at sea level to 1,000m asl. Females lay 3–8 eggs per clutch.

Philippine Bronzeback Snake ■ *Dendrelaphis philippinensis*
SVL 900mm; TL 1,200mm (e)

DESCRIPTION Long, slender, agile snake with brown dorsum. Head distinct from neck, with 6–7 temporal scales. Eyes large with round pupils. Upper labials: nine, lower labials: 9–11. Postocular stripe extends to neck and merges with longitudinal stripe on body; 2–6 black longitudinal stripes at mid-body. Black ventrolateral line. Dorsal scales smooth; 13 scale rows at mid-body. Ventral pale yellowish-green; ventrals: 162–170 (males) to 161–172 (females); 94–108 subcaudals. Anal plate divided. Tail 25–29 per cent of TL.
DISTRIBUTION Basilan, Bohol, Camiguin Sur, Catanduanes, Cebu, Dinagat, Kalotkot, Leyte, Luzon (Albay), Mindanao, Polillo, Samar, Siargao, Siquijor. **HABITS AND HABITAT** Diurnal and mainly arboreal. Feeds on geckos and frogs.

Philippine Whip Snake

■ *Dryophiops philippina*
SVL 548mm; TL 806mm

DESCRIPTION Slender snake. Dorsal colour ranges from light grey to brown. Head elongated; snout rounded and distinct from neck. Eyes large with slightly oblong pupils. Small brown dots on top of head and oblong marking with dark border on neck. One preocular, two postoculars. Upper labials: nine, fourth to sixth in contact with eye, lower labials: nine. Dorsal scales smooth; some edged black. Interstitial skin white, appearing as series of short parallel lines. **DISTRIBUTION** Luzon, Marinduque, Mindanao, Mindoro, Panay, Romblon, Sibuyan, Samar. **HABITS AND HABITAT** Arboreal, occurring in forests and disturbed areas at sea level to 500m asl. Feeds on small lizards such as *Lipinia* spp. Hatchlings 210–215mm TL.

Red Whip Snake ▪ *Dryophiops rubescens* SVL 585mm; TL 840mm

DESCRIPTION Slender snake with elongated, depressed head. Brown stripe from snout through eye to neck. Dorsum varies from light greyish-brown to reddish-brown with dark spots. One preocular, two postoculars, one loreal, long and narrow. Upper labials: nine, fourth to sixth in contact with eye, lower labials: 10–11. Lower labials and chin white. Dorsal scales smooth; 15 scale rows at mid-body. Interstitial skin white, appearing as series of short parallel lines. Ventrals: 186–199. Subcaudals: 111–136. Anal plate divded. Tail about 30 per cent of TL. **DISTRIBUTION** Coron, Lagen, Miniloc, Palawan. **HABITS AND HABITAT** Arboreal and diurnal. Feeds mainly on lizards such as geckos and skinks.

Luzon Reed Snake ■ *Calamaria bitorques* SVL 520mm; TL 540mm

DESCRIPTION Dorsum yellowish-brown to greyish-olive with scattered black spots on body, especially on anterior part. Dark cross-bands behind head: 2–6. Head not distinct from body. Upper labials: five, third and fourth in contact with eye; five lower labial scales. Upper labials cream without spots. Mental scale in contact with anterior chin-shields. Ventral pale yellow with or without dark brown bands. Ventrals: 157–175. Subcaudal pale yellow with or without median dark brown stripe. Subcaudals: 15–17. Tail to TL ratio: 3.9–8.6 per cent. **DISTRIBUTION** Luzon, Panay. **HABITS AND HABITAT** Fossorial and nocturnal. Usually found under logs or leaf litter in forests.

Gervais' Reed Snake ▪ *Calamaria gervaisii* TL 321mm ⓔ

DESCRIPTION Dorsum uniform brown. Dorsal scales smooth, with dark spots forming longitudinal rows. Head not distinct from neck, with rounded snout. Upper labials: six, third and fourth in contact with eye, lower labials: six. Labials and chin yellow. Ventrals: 133–163 (males), 143–189 (females). Subcaudals: 12–17 (males), 15–20 (females). Subcaudal has median dark brown stripe. **DISTRIBUTION** Basilan, Camiguin Norte, Catanduanes, Cebu, Basilan, Luzon, Masbate, Mindanao, Mindoro, Negros, Panay, Polillo, Romblon, Tablas. **HABITS AND HABITAT** Fossorial and nocturnal. Commonly seen under leaf litter or pots in urban gardens. Females lay 3–6 eggs per clutch.

Variable Reed Snake ▪ *Calamaria lumbricoidea* TL 642mm

DESCRIPTION Large reed snake with females attaining greater length than males. Dorsum dark brown to black with pale yellow cross-bands and orange spots. Dorsal head colour variable – pale yellow, orange or black. Labials and chin pale yellow. Mental scale in contact with anterior chin-shields. Ventral yellow with dark cross-bands, each more than one ventral scale wide. Philippines populations – ventrals: 165–176 (males), 188–229 (females); subcaudals: 22–27 (males), 14–20 (females). Tail to TL ratio: 6.3–11.4 per cent (males); 3.9–8.3 per cent (females). **DISTRIBUTION** Basilan, Biliran, Bohol, Camiguin Sur, Dinagat, Leyte, Mindanao. **HABITS AND HABITAT** Fossorial and nocturnal. Usually found under logs or leaf litter in forests.

Sulu Reed Snake ■ *Calamaria suluensis* TL 295mm

DESCRIPTION Small reed snake with iridescent brown dorsum. Eyes large. Scales of first dorsal scale row have white centres, forming stripe. Upper labials: six, third and fourth

in contact with eye, lower labials: six. Mental scale in contact with anterior chin-shields. Ventral yellow, with or without dark brown bands. Ventrals: 129–138 (males), 142–168 (females). Subcaudal has median dark brown stripe. Subcaudals: 18–20 (males), 14–26 (females). Tail to TL ratio: 7.9–10.4 per cent (males); 6.4–10.9 per cent (females). **DISTRIBUTION** Mapun, Tawi-Tawi. **HABITS AND HABITAT** Fossorial and nocturnal. Usually found under logs or leaf litter in forests.

McNamara's Burrowing Snake
■ *Pseudorabdion mcnamarae* SVL 220mm; TL 242mm ⓔ

DESCRIPTION Small snake with short tail. Head tapering and not distinct from neck. Dorsum iridescent reddish-brown to blackish-brown. Ocular shield usually not fused with other surrounding scales, loreal scale present, and prefrontal scale not in contact with upper labial scales. Yellow nuchal collar on young individuals but fades with age. Ventral off-white or pale yellow. Ventrals: 126–135 (males); 136–145 (females). Subcaudals: 26–29 (males); 17–23 (females). Tail to TL ratio: 11–12.3 per cent (males); 8.3–9.6 per cent (females). Luzon populations (illustrated) may be distinct species from western Visayas.

DISTRIBUTION Biliran, Cebu, Luzon, Masbate, Negros, Panay, Sibuyan, Tablas. **HABITS AND HABITAT** Semifossorial. Inhabits primary and secondary forests at 300–1,600m asl. Individuals usually seen under rotten logs, leaf litter and coconut husks along forest trails after strong rain. Predates on earthworms and has been documented to be predated by triangle-spotted snakes.

Mountain Burrowing Snake ■ *Pseudorabdion montanum* TL 531mm

DESCRIPTION Large *Pseudorabdion* snake with short tail. Head tapering and not distinct from neck. Preocular and loreal scales absent, supraocular and postocular scales usually fused together, prefrontal scale in contact with upper labial scales, frontal scale not in contact with eye, and fourth upper labial not in contact with parietal. Dorsum iridescent reddish-brown. Each dorsal scale on first row has light centre and dark edges. Ventrals: 146–148 (males); 154–161 (females). Subcaudals: 28 (males); 21–24 (females). **DISTRIBUTION** Cebu, Negros. **HABITS AND HABITAT** Semifossorial. Inhabits primary and secondary forests to 1,200m asl. Individuals usually seen under rotten logs, leaf litter and coconut husks, or along forest trails after strong rain. Predates on earthworms.

Visayan Burrowing Snake ■ *Pseudorabdion oxycephalum*
SVL 260mm; TL282mm

DESCRIPTION Small snake with short tail. Head tapering and not distinct from neck. Preocular and loreal scales absent, supraocular and postocular scales usually fused together, prefrontal scale in contact with two upper labial scales, frontal scale not in contact with eye, and fourth upper labial in contact with lower anterior of parietal. Dorsum iridescent dark reddish-brown to dark grey. Each dorsal scale on first row has dark centre and light edges. Ventral same colour as dorsal, but with light edges posteriorly. Ventrals: 132–144 (males); 144–157 (females). Subcaudals: 22–24 (males); 16–17 (females). Tail to TL ratio: 10.8–12.9 per cent (males); 6.1–8.2 per cent (females). **DISTRIBUTION** Cebu, Luzon, Mindanao, Masbate, Negros, Panay. **HABITS AND HABITAT** Semifossorial. Inhabits primary and secondary forests from sea level to 750m asl. Individuals usually seen under rotten logs, leaf litter and coconut husks, or along forest trails after strong rain. Predates on earthworms. Females lay 2–3 eggs per clutch.

Philippine Blunt-headed Cat Snake

■ *Boiga angulata* SVL 1,100mm; TL 1,480mm ⓔ

DESCRIPTION Dorsum brown with darker brown to greyish-brown cross-bands widening laterally, and white blotches on lower lateral body. Snout short and blunt. Head distinct from neck. Eyes large, with vertical pupils, and light grey irises. One preocular, two postoculars and one loreal. Upper labials: eight, third–fifth in contact with eye, lower labials: 10. Ventral scales: 254–267; dorsal scales smooth and 19 scale rows at mid-body; paired subcaudal scales: 126–153. **DISTRIBUTION** Bohol, Catanduanes, Inampulugan, Leyte, Luzon, Mindanao, Negros, Panay, Polillo, Samara, Tablas. **HABITS AND HABITAT** Arboreal and nocturnal. Inhabits primary and secondary forests at 0–2,500m asl. Usually seen sleeping on tree branches by day or while actively foraging for prey at night.

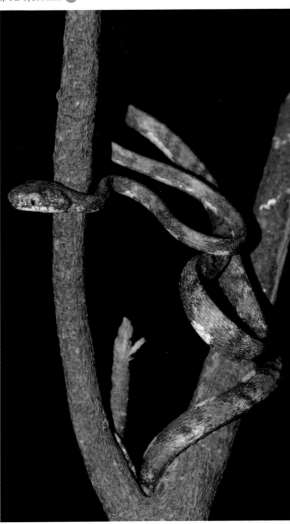

Dog-toothed Cat Snake ■ *Boiga cynodon* SVL 1,880mm; TL 2,390mm

DESCRIPTION Typical appearance of this large snake: brown or grey with irregular blotches bordered with black. Patternless morphs ranging from brown to orange also documented. Head distinct from neck. Eyes large with brownish-orange irises. Black bar behind eye. One preocular, two postoculars and one loreal. Upper labials: 8–9, fourth to sixth in contact with eye, lower labials: 13–15, eighth anterior to centre of eye. Vertebral scales enlarged and hexagonal in shape. Ventral scales: 248–290, dorsal scale rows at midbody: 23, subcaudal scales: 114–157. **DISTRIBUTION** Basilan, Bohol, Calayan, Camiguin Norte, Carabao, Culion, Dinagat, Inampulugan, Leyte, Lubang, Luzon, Mindanao, Negros, Palawan, Pan de Azucar, Panay, Polillo, Romblon, Sibutu, Siquijor, Tablas, Tawi-Tawi. **HABITS AND HABITAT** Arboreal and nocturnal. Inhabits primary and secondary forests at 0–600m asl. Feeds primarily on birds and to lesser extent birds' eggs, bats, lizards, frogs and rodents. Females lay 6–12 eggs per clutch.

Samar

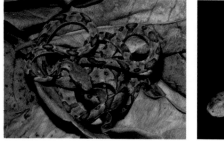

Luzon

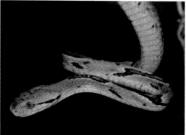

Mindanao

Luzon Mangrove Snake ■ *Boiga dendrophila divergens*
SVL 1,110mm; TL 1,370mm

DESCRIPTION Large snake with laterally compressed body. Head large, blunt and distinct from neck. Scales on lateral part of head have yellow markings. Eyes large with vertical pupils. Dorsum dark bluish-grey with 85–79 narrow yellow or light blue cross-bands. Upper labials: eight, third to fifth in contact with eye, lower labials: 10, five in contact with anterior chin-shields. Ventral scales: 219–228, subcaudals: 80–87. **DISTRIBUTION** Calayan, Luzon, Polillo. **HABITS AND HABITAT** Arboreal and nocturnal. Often seen on tree branches near waterbodies such as mangroves, rivers and forest stream. Predates on small vertebrates including lizards, frogs and birds.

Mindanao Mangrove Snake
■ *Boiga dendrophila latifasciata* SVL 962mm; TL 1,220mm

DESCRIPTION Robust black snake with laterally compressed body. Light yellow cross-bands on dorsum at least two scales wide and becoming wider laterally. Upper labials: eight, third to fifth in contact with eye, lower labials: 10, four in contact with anterior chin-shields. Ventral scales: 207–226, subcaudals: 93–102. **DISTRIBUTION** Bohol, Leyte, Mindanao, Samar, Siargao. **HABITS AND HABITAT** Arboreal and nocturnal. Usually seen sleeping on branches of trees along riverbanks and mangrove forests by day. Predates on small vertebrates, including bats, lizards, frogs and birds.

Palawan Mangrove Snake ■ *Boiga dendrophila multicincta*

SVL 900mm; TL 1,160mm 🄴

DESCRIPTION Black dorsum with 58–84 narrow yellow cross-bands. Dorsal head black with or without yellow spots. Scales on lateral head have yellow markings. Body laterally compressed and with smooth scales. Ventral scales: 220–240, subcaudals: 105–115. Locally known as *Binturan*. **DISTRIBUTION** Balabac, Palawan. **HABITS AND HABITAT** Arboreal and nocturnal. Usually seen sleeping on branches of trees along riverbanks and mangrove forests by day. An individual was seen being predated by a King Cobra (p. 157) in mangrove area on Palawan Island.

White-spotted Cat Snake ■ *Boiga drapiezii* SVL 1,500mm; TL 2,000mm

DESCRIPTION Long, slender snake with laterally compressed body. Head distinct from neck, and snout short and blunt. Dorsal head has black dots. Colour and pattern highly variable, from greyish to brownish-orange with vertical bars. Vertebral scales enlarged. Dorsal scales smooth and 19 scale rows at mid-body. Ventral scales: 258–287, subcaudal scales: 150–173. **DISTRIBUTION** Mindanao, Sibutu, Tawi-Tawi. **HABITS AND HABITAT** Arboreal and nocturnal. Inhabits primary and secondary forests at 80–900m asl. Predates on frogs and lizards.

Philippine Cat Snake ■ *Boiga philippina* SVL 895mm; TL 1,180mm ⓔ

DESCRIPTION Dorsum brownish-orange, with or without narrow chevron cross-bands. Head distinct from neck and snout short and blunt. Two preoculars, one loreal and two postoculars. Upper labials: 8–9, lower labials: 12, eighth posterior to centre of eye. Vertebral scales enlarged. Dorsal scale rows at mid-body: 19. Anal plate divided, ventral scales: 250–266, subcaudal scales: 126–133. **DISTRIBUTION** Babuyan Claro, Luzon. **HABITS AND HABITAT** Arboreal and nocturnal. Inhabits forests and agroforests at 50–800m asl. Little known about preferred prey items.

Schultze's Blunt-headed Cat Snake

■ *Boiga schultzei* SVL 956mm; TL 1,330mm ⓔ

DESCRIPTION Dorsum brown with about 70 transverse blotches, not widening laterally, and/or narrow dark brown cross-bands. Head distinct from neck, and snout short and blunt. One preocular, one loreal and two postoculars. Upper labials: 7–8. Dorsal scale rows at mid-body: 19. Anal plate single, ventral scales: 250–276, subcaudal scales: 114–163. **DISTRIBUTION** Palawan. **HABITS AND HABITAT** Arboreal and nocturnal. Inhabits secondary forests and disturbed areas at sea level to 200m asl.

Philippine Red-tailed Ratsnake

■ *Coelognathus erythrurus erythrurus* SVL 1,060mm; TL 1,370mm

DESCRIPTION Dorsum of adults brown to reddish-brown anteriorly and dark brown posteriorly. Head elongated and distinct from neck. One preocular, two postoculars, one loreal, and two anterior temporals plus two posteriar temporals. Upper labials: nine, fourth–sixth in contact with eye, lower labials: 11. Dorsal scales keeled except outer rows, which are smooth. Ventrals: 211–220 (males), 216–227 (females). Subcaudals: 96–104 (males), 90–107 (females). Hatchings and juveniles olive dorsum with series of white cross-bands and bright reddish tail. **DISTRIBUTION** Basilan, Bohol, Bongao, Camiguin Sur, Dinagat, Jolo, Leyte, Mindanao, Pacijan, Poro, Samar, Siasi. **HABITS AND HABITAT** Diurnal and terrestrial. Occurs at sea level to 850m asl. Mainly predates on rodents.

Adult

Hatchling

Luzon Red-tailed Ratsnake ■ *Coelognathus erythrurus manillensis*
SVL 1,220mm; TL 1,560mm ⓔ

Adult

DESCRIPTION Dorsum uniform light to reddish-brown. Head elongated and distinct from neck. One preocular, two postoculars, one loreal, and two anterior temporals and two posterior temporals. Upper labials: nine, fourth to sixth in contact with eye, lower labials: 11. Ventrals: 211–217, subcaudals: 91–95. Dorsum of hatchlings and juveniles light brown to olive-brown anteriorly and reddish-brown posteriorly. Short, diagonal black stripe behind eye and black stripe on neck; fade with age. **DISTRIBUTION** Batan, Barit, Calayan, Dalupiri, Guinahoan, Lahuy, Luzon, Mindoro, Polillo; Catanduanes(?). **HABITS AND HABITAT** Diurnal and terrestrial. Common in urban gardens and agricultural areas at sea level to more than 1,000m asl. Mainly feeds on rodents. **NOTE** Population on Catanduanes Island resembles western Visayas subspecies, but is tentatively referred to this species.

Hatchling

Philippine Grey-tailed Ratsnake

■ *Coelognathus erythrurus psephenourus* SVL 1,200mm; TL 1,600mm

DESCRIPTION Large, slender, non-venomous snake. Dorsum light brown to olive-brown anteriorly. Posterior body and tail dark brown. Dorsal scales weakly keeled except for outer scale rows, which are smooth; 21 transverse scale row at mid-body. Ventral colour white or cream. Head elongated and distinct from neck. Eyes large with round pupils. One preocular, two postoculars, one loreal, and two anterior temporals and two posterior temporals. Upper labials: nine, fourth to sixth in contact with eye, lower labials: 11. Ventrals: 214–230. Subcaudals: 90–105. Juveniles have series of short white bars on dorsal body. **DISTRIBUTION** Cebu, Guimaras, Inampulugan, Masbate, Negros, Panay, Siquijor, Tablas. **HABITS AND HABITAT** Diurnal and terrestrial. Commonly seen in urban gardens and agricultural areas from sea level to 600m asl. Mainly predates on rodents.

Hatchling

Adult

Western Philippine Ratsnake ■ *Coelognathus philippinus*
SVL 1,170mm; TL 1,500mm (e)

DESCRIPTION Moderate-sized snake with cylindrical body. Dorsum brown anteriorly and dark reddish-brown posteriorly. Head elongated and distinct from neck. Eyes large with round pupils. One black stripe below and behind each eye. Longer black stripe starting from lower posterior temporal to neck. One loreal, one preocular, two postoculars, two anterior and two posterior temporals. Upper labials: nine, fourth to sixth in contact with eye, lower labials: 11. Dorsal scales keeled and 21 scale rows at mid-body. Ventrals: 223–227 (males), 231–238 (females). Subcaudals: 106–114 (males), 102–111 (females). Tail length about 21.5 per cent of TL. **DISTRIBUTION** Balabac, Bongao, Culion, Palawan, Sanga-Sanga, Sibutu, Tawi-Tawi. **HABITS AND HABITAT** Diurnal and terrestrial. Common in lowland areas. Feeds mainly on rodents.

Red-tailed Green Ratsnake ■ *Gonyosoma oxycephalum*
SVL 1,800mm; TL 2,400mm

DESCRIPTION Large snake with laterally compressed body. Head narrow and slightly distinct from neck. Broad black stripe from nasal through eye to temple. One preocular, two postoculars and one loreal. Upper labials: 8–11, lower labials: 12–15. Dorsal uniform green, yellowish-green or brown. Dorsal scales smooth or weakly keeled. Interstitial skin black, resulting in net-like pattern on body. Dorsal tail brown, grey or reddish-brown. Ventral scales light green. **DISTRIBUTION** Balabac, Batan, Bohol, Bongao, Calayan, Camiguin Norte, Dinagat, Leyte, Lubang, Luzon, Marinduque, Mindanao, Negros, Palawan, Panay, Sabtang, Sibuyan. **HABITS AND HABITAT** Arboreal and diurnal. Preys on birds, bats, rodents and lizards. When threatened, neck area is inflated to appear larger. Occurs in forests and forest edges at sea level to 750m asl. Females lay 3–12 eggs per clutch. Hatchlings 430–550mm TL.

Common Wolf Snake ■ *Lycodon capucinus* SVL 664mm; TL 781mm

DESCRIPTION Head depressed and distinct from neck. Dorsum dark brown to grey with irregular network formed by white-edged scales. Usually broad white nuchal band. Eyes small with vertical pupils. One preocular, two postoculars, one loreal and 1+2 or 2+3 temporals. Upper labials: nine, third to fifth in contact with eye, lower labials: 10. Dorsal scales smooth and 17 scale rows at mid-body. Ventrals: 190–210. Subcaudals: 63–74. Anal plate divided. Tail long, terminating in sharp point. Tail to TL ratio: 13–20 per cent. **DISTRIBUTION** Bantayan, Bohol, Camiguin Sur, Carabao, Cebu, Cuyo, Dinagat, Leyte, Luzon, Masbate, Mindanao, Mindoro, Negros, Palawan, Panay, Romblon, Samar, Semirara, Tablas. **HABITS AND HABITAT** Nocturnal and terrestrial. Often seen hiding in or around houses and agricultural areas. Mainly predates on house geckos and occasionally on mice. Females lay 3–11 eggs per clutch. Hatchlings 140–197mm TL. **NOTE** Probably introduced species due to widespread albeit disjunct distribution in the Philippines.

Dumeril's Wolf Snake ■ *Lycodon dumerilii* SVL 340mm

DESCRIPTION Dorsum dark grey to black with 15–19 white or yellow cross-bands on body. Head distinct from neck. Upper labials: 8–9, fourth and fifth in contact with eye.

Loreal scale distinct or fused with lower preocular. Dorsal scales smooth and 17 scale rows at mid-body. Ventrals: 195–221. Subcaudals: 111–120. Anal plate single. Tail to TL ratio about 27 per cent. Hatchlings and juveniles have nuchal collar that fades with age. **DISTRIBUTION** Basilan, Dinagat, Leyte, Mindanao, Samar, Siargao. **HABITS AND HABITAT** Occurs in primary and secondary forests at sea level to 800m asl. Has been seen on the ground while hunting for lizards.

Juvenile

Adult

Müller's Wolf Snake ◾ *Lycodon muelleri* SVL 547mm

DESCRIPTION Slender snake with cylindrical body. Head depressed, distinct from neck and with network of narrow, irregular lines. Dorsum reddish-brown with 51–64 light cross-bands on body and 28–31 light cross-bands on tail. Dorsal scales smooth and 17 scale rows at mid-body. Ventrals: 203–211. Subcaudals: 112–127 pairs. Tail long and tapering. **DISTRIBUTION** Batan, Catanduanes, Lahuy, Luzon, Marinduque, Mindoro, Polillo. **HABITS AND HABITAT** Occurs in primary and secondary forests at sea level to 1,235m asl. Usually seen on branches of trees or epiphytes.

Palawan Wolf Snake ■ *Lycodon philippinus* SVL 370mm; TL 485mm

DESCRIPTION Dorsum dark brown to black with median cream-coloured stripe. Second cream stripe on fourth scale row, followed by dark brown stripe on third scale row. Parietals edged with cream posteriorly. One preocular or fused with supraocular, three postoculars and one loreal, in contact with eye. Upper labials: seven, third and fourth in contact with eye, lower labials: seven. Labials pale yellow. Dorsal scales smooth, and 15 scale rows at mid-body. Ventral and subcaudal scales strongly keeled. Ventrals: 216–225. Subcaudals: 87–116. Anal plate single. **DISTRIBUTION** Balabac, Palawan. **HABITS AND HABITAT** Nocturnal and arboreal. Occurs in primary and secondary forests. Little known about its natural history.

Seale's Wolf Snake ■ *Lycodon sealei* SVL 416mm

DESCRIPTION Dorsum uniform lavender-grey. Median dorsal scales weakly keeled. Preocular absent, 1–2 postoculars, loreal elongated, and 1+2 or 2+2 temporals. Upper labials: eight, third to fifth in contact with eye, lower labials: nine. Ventrals: 198–211. Subcaudals: 60–68. Dorsal scale rows at mid-body: 17. Anal plate divided. Hatchlings and juveniles have broad white cross-bands on dorsum. **DISTRIBUTION** Palawan. **HABITS AND HABITAT** Occurs in primary and secondary forests at sea level to 1,500m asl. Usually seen on the ground while hunting for prey such as skinks.

Northern Philippine Short-headed Snake

▪ *Oligodon ancorus* SVL 483mm; TL 574mm ⓔ

DESCRIPTION Dorsum reddish-brown to greyish-brown, with 14–22 black-edged blotches and faint reddish-brown vertebral streak. Dark 'Y'-shaped marking may be connected to dark interocular cross-band. Dark diagonal temporal streak. One preocular, two postoculars, one loreal, rectangular in shape, and 1+2 or 2+2 temporals. Upper labials: seven, third and fourth in contact with eye, lower labials: 7–8. Dorsal scales smooth, and 17 scale rows at mid-body. Ventrals: 147–171. Subcaudals: 33–45. Anal plate single. Hatchlings and juveniles have light brown dorsum with black blotches and pale orange ventrals. **DISTRIBUTION** Luzon, Marinduque, Mindoro. **HABITS AND HABITAT** Terrestrial and noctural, but seen basking in an open area of a garden adjacent to a secondary forest in early afternoon. Inhabits primary and secondary forests at sea level to 600m asl.

Adult

Juvenile

Spotted-bellied Short-headed Snake

■ *Oligodon modestus* SVL 332mm; TL 377mm

DESCRIPTION Small snake with short head and short tail. Head not distinct from neck. Dorsum dark brown with reddish-brown vertebral stripe and no prominent blotches. Dark brown interocular and dorsal head cross-band. Nuchal area has broad light brown band. One preocular, one postocular, loreal absent, and 1+2 or 1+3 temporals. Upper labials: 5–6, third in contact with eye, lower labials: 6–7. Dorsal scales smooth, and 15 scale rows at mid-body. Ventral yellowish with brown or black rectangular spots. Ventrals: 158–173 (males), 170–176 (females). Subcaudals: 36–44 (males), 27–37 (females). Anal plate single. Tail to TL ratio 12–16 per cent. **DISTRIBUTION** Negros, Panay, Tablas. **HABITS AND HABITAT** Terrestrial and nocturnal. Inhabits primary and secondary forests at sea level to 950m asl. Seen basking on open forest patch in early afternoon, and hunting for frog (*Platymantis* sp.) in forest edge at noon. **NOTE** Records from Luzon and Mindanao probably misidentified.

Palawan Short-headed Snake ■ *Oligodon notospilus*
SVL 292mm; TL 345mm ⓔ

DESCRIPTION Dorsum grey to brown with black-edged, light brown spots. Dorsal head lighter colour than dorsum, with two dark, chevron-shaped markings. One preocular, two postoculars, one loreal, and 1+1 or 1+2 temporals. Upper labials: seven, third and fourth in contact with eye, lower labials: 7–8. Dorsal scales smooth, and 15 scale rows at mid-body. Lateral body has scattered white dots. Ventral yellowish without markings. Ventrals: 136–143. Subcaudals: 35–43. Anal plate single. Tail ends in sharp point. **DISTRIBUTION** Balabac, Busuanga, Calauit, Palawan. **HABITS AND HABITAT** Terrestrial and nocturnal. Inhabits primary and secondary forests. Biology little known.

Philippine Smooth-scaled Mountain Ratsnake
■ *Ptyas luzonensis* SVL 1,950mm; TL 2,600mm

DESCRIPTION Large snake with slightly compressed body and black tail. Head elongated and distinct from neck. Dorsum brown with black-edged scales creating net-like pattern. Eyes large with round pupils. One or two preoculars, 2–3 postoculars, one loreal, and 2+2 or 2+3 temporals. Upper labials: eight, third to fifth or fourth to fifth in contact with eye, lower labials: 7–10. Anterior third of dorsal body has 12–14 scales per row. Smooth mid-body scales. Ventral variable: pale yellow, pale orange, cream or grey anteriorly, and dark olive-brown to dark grey posteriorly. Ventrals: 191–216. Paired subcaudals: 101–125. Anal plate divided. Tail to TL ratio: 22–26 per cent. **DISTRIBUTION** Camiguin Norte, Catanduanes, Leyte, Luzon, Negros, Panay, Polillo. **HABITS AND HABITAT** Semi-arboreal and diurnal. Inhabits secondary and primary forests at sea level to 1,100m asl. Often seen on forest floors and river or stream banks by day, and sleeping on horizontal branches at night. **NOTE** Slithers towards people to escape when threatened. Occasionally mistaken for the King Cobra (p. 157).

Philippine Cave Snake ■ *Stegonotus muelleri*
SVL 1,680mm; TL 2,070mm ⓔ

DESCRIPTION Dorsum uniform brown or grey. Head depressed and distinct from neck. Two preoculars, two postoculars, one loreal, rectangular. Upper labials: nine, fourth and fifth in contact with eye, 2+3 temporals. Eyes small with vertical pupils. Dorsal scales smooth, and 17 scale rows at mid-body. Labials, throat and ventral dirty-white or pale yellow. Ventrals: 220–232. Subcaudals: 81–100 pairs. Tail long and tapering.
DISTRIBUTION Bohol, Dinagat, Leyte, Mindanao, Samar. **HABITS AND HABITAT** Terrestrial and nocturnal. Inhabits primary and secondary forests at sea level to 1,000 asl. Commonly seen inside caves.

White-lined Keelback Snake ■ *Rhabdophis auriculatus auriculatus*
SVL 379mm; TL 524mm

DESCRIPTION Small, slender snake with short, blunt head. Dorsum brown or grey with lighter median stripe and lateral body stripe on outer row. Lateral stripe is usually not in contact with light blotch behind eye. Two preoculars, two postoculars, one loreal, and 2+3 temporals. Upper labials: 8–9, third to fifth in contact with eye, lower labials: 9–10. Ventral body scales black. Ventrals: 143–160. Subcaudals: 71–87. Anal plate divided. **DISTRIBUTION** Dinagat, Leyte, Mindanao, Samar. **HABITS AND HABITAT** Terrestrial and diurnal. Inhabits forests and modified areas at 75–2,100m asl. Usually seen on forest floors and in riparian habitats. Feeds on frogs and frogs' eggs.

Speckle-bellied Keelback Snake

■ *Rhabdophis chrysargos* SVL 625mm; TL 825mm

DESCRIPTION Dorsal body greenish-brown to greyish-brown. Head grey, elongated and distinct from neck. Eyes large with round pupils. One preocular, three postoculars and one loreal. Labials and throat dirty-white. Upper labials: nine, fourth to sixth in contact with eye, lower labials: 11. Sixth labial scale not in contact with temporal scale. Dorsal scales strongly keeled and 19 scale rows at mid-body. Ventrals cream or pale yellow; grey or light brown on edges with dark spots. Ventrals: 150–160. Subcaudals: 80–90. Anal plate divided. Hatchlings and juveniles have white nuchal collar. **DISTRIBUTION** Balabac, Busuanga, Culion, Dumaran, Palawan. **HABITS AND HABITAT** Terrestrial and diurnal. Often seen near waterbodies such as streams in forests, and disturbed areas bordering forests at 200–1,700m asl. Predates primarily on frogs and toads, including the Philippine Toad *Ingerophrynus philippinicus* and occasionally on fish.

Adult

Juvenile

Striped Keelback Snake ▪ *Rhabdophis lineatus* SVL 530mm; TL 690mm ⓔ

DESCRIPTION Dorsum uniform greyish-brown. Distinct light stripe from rostral to upper labial scales. Head distinct from neck. Two preoculars, three postoculars and one loreal. Upper labials: eight, fourth and fifth in contact with eye, lower labials: nine. Sixth upper labial in contact with anterior temporal. Dorsal scales strongly keeled except outer scale row, which is not keeled or weakly so, and 19 scale rows at mid-body. Ventral cream or pale yellow. Ventrals: 132–148. Subcaudals: 64–71. Subcaudal has zigzag line. Anal plate divided. Hatchlings and juveniles reddish-brown with white nuchal collar. Dorsum has regularly spaced dark spots. **DISTRIBUTION** Basilan, Biliran, Bohol, Dinagat, Leyte, Mindanao, Samar. **HABITS AND HABITAT** Terrestrial and diurnal. Strongly associated with riparian habitats. Usually found under logs and leaf litter. Occurs at sea level to 1,300m asl.

Negros Spotted Water Snake ■ *Tropidonophis negrosensis*
SVL 555mm; TL 730mm ⓔ

DESCRIPTION Slender snake with cylindrical body. Head elongated and distinct from neck. Dorsum reddish-brown to olive with series of dark spots. Lateral body has row of dark spots. Eyes large with round pupils. One preocular, 3–4 postoculars, one loreal, and 2+3 or 1+3 temporals. Upper labials: nine, fourth to sixth in contact with eye, lower labials: 10. Ventral pinkish-white or pale yellow with small black spots on each scale. Ventrals: 162–169. Subcaudals 91–97. Anal plate divided. Tail to TL ratio 24–28 per cent. **DISTRIBUTION** Cebu, Masbate, Mindoro, Negros, Pan de Azucar, Panay, Sicogon, Siquijor. **HABITS AND HABITAT** Terrestrial. Active by day and night. Inhabits forests near waterbodies such as rivers and streams at sea level to 1,200m asl. Predates on ground-dwelling frogs such as *Platymantis* sp.

Luzon Keelback Snake ■ *Tropidonophis spilogaster*
SVL 535mm; TL 735mm

DESCRIPTION Dorsal body greyish-brown with three longitudinal stripes or rows of black spots at regular intervals. Distinct light nuchal spot. Dorsal scales strongly keeled except outer row, which may not be keeled or is weakly so, and 17 scale rows at mid-body. Two preoculars, three postoculars, one loreal, and 2+2 or 2+3 temporals. Upper labials: nine, fourth to sixth in contact with eye, lower labials: 10. Ventral cream with small dots on edges. Ventrals: 147–155. Subcaudals: 80–91. Anal plate divided. Hatchlings and juveniles more brightly coloured than adults. **DISTRIBUTION** Batan, Camiguin Norte, Catanduanes, Luzon, Polillo. **HABITS AND HABITAT** Terrestrial and diurnal. Inhabits primary and secondary forests at sea level to 1,200m asl. Often seen in agricultural areas near streams. Mainly predates on frogs.

Palawan Yellow-striped Snake ■ *Sibynophis bivittatus* SVL 370mm

DESCRIPTION Dorsum dark brown with pair of pale yellow dorsolateral stripes from behind posterior temporals to tail-tip. Pale yellow interocular blotch. Upper labial scales have large white spots. Eyes large with round pupils. One preocular, two postoculars, one loreal, and 2+2 temporals. Upper labials: eight (rarely nine), third to fifth or fourth to fifth in contact with eye, lower labials: nine. Ventral colour pale greenish-yellow without spots. Ventrals: 145–155. Subcaudals: 110–112. Anal plate divided. Tail slender and long. **DISTRIBUTION** Busuanga, Culion, Dumaran, Palawan. **HABITS AND HABITAT** Terrestrial and diurnal. Inhabits primary and secondary forests at sea level to 975m asl. Mainly predates on lizards.

CYCLOCORIDAE (CYCLOCORIDS)
This Philippine-endemic snake family originated 25–35 million years ago and currently occurs across the archipelago. It contains five genera (*Cyclocorus, Hologerrhum, Levitonius, Myersophis* and *Oxyrhabdium*) and 11 taxa.

Alcala's Triangle-spotted Snake

■ *Cyclocorus lineatus alcalai* SVL 432mm; TL 503mm (e)

DESCRIPTION Dorsum reddish to dark brown with three faint dark stripes. Dark brown markings on top of head and behind eye. Head slightly distinct from neck. Eyes small with round pupils. Two preoculars, two postoculars and one loreal. Upper labials: eight, third to fifth in contact with eye, lower labials: 8–9. Ventral cream or off-white with triangle-shaped markings. Subcaudals: 42–53 (males), 33–44 (females). Tail to TL ratio: 23.5–29.6 per cent (males), 15.2–22.3 per cent (females). **DISTRIBUTION** Cebu, Guimaras, Inampulugan, Negros, Panay, Sibuyan, Tablas. **HABITS AND HABITAT** Nocturnal and semifossorial. Occurs in forests and agricultural areas at sea level to 1,200m asl. Usually seen under logs or piles of coconut husks. Feeds on small snakes and skinks. Females lay 3–6 eggs per clutch under logs.

Luzon Triangle-spotted Snake

▪ *Cyclocorus lineatus lineatus* 353mm; TL 465mm ⓔ

DESCRIPTION Small snake with cylindrical body and small head. Eyes small with round pupils. Dorsum reddish-brown to grey with median dark brown stripe. Dark brown stripe on dorsal head and two postocular stripes. Lateral dorsal body brown or grey. Two preoculars, two postoculars, one loreal, and 1+2 or 2+2 temporals. Upper labials: eight, third to fifth in contact with eye. Dorsal scales smooth and 17 scale rows at mid-body. Ventral cream with triangle-shaped spots. Prominent white spots along edges of ventral body scales. Ventrals: 142–157 (males), 146–163 (females). Subcaudals: 52–59 (males), 42–48 (females). Tail to TL ratio: 29.5–37.1 per cent (males), 19.6–26.2 per cent (females). Anal plate single. **DISTRIBUTION** Calayan, Camiguin Norte, Catanduanes, Lubang, Luzon, Marinduque, Mindoro, Polillo. **HABITS AND HABITAT** Nocturnal and semifossorial. Inhabits forests at sea level to 1,400m asl.

Panay White-lipped Snake

■ *Hologerrhum dermali*
SVL 327mm; TL 420mm

DESCRIPTION Philippine-endemic genus known to contain two species. Small snake with reddish-brown head slightly distinct from neck. Eyes small with round pupils. Two preoculars, two postoculars, one loreal, eight upper labials and eight lower labials. Dorsum brown with 8–17 pairs of black spots. Broad, dark brown vertebral stripe on neck area may be present. Upper lip bright white. Ventral scales pale yellow with black stripe in middle. Ventrals: 139–149. Subcaudals: 49–62. **DISTRIBUTION** Panay, Sibuyan. **HABITS AND HABITAT** Terrestrial and diurnal, occurring in forests at 410–1510m asl. Has been seen on forest floors and under rocks in dry stream or river beds.

Luzon White-lipped Snake ■ *Hologerrhum philippinum*
SVL 347mm; TL 443mm

DESCRIPTION Rear-fanged snake with pair of enlarged, grooved fangs in upper jaw. Dorsal reddish-brown. Head slightly distinct from neck. Eyes small with round pupils. Body cylindrical with smooth dorsal scales. Dorsum brown with 12–30 pairs of black spots. Broad, dark brown vertebral stripe on neck area may be present. Upper lip pale yellow or white. Ventral scales orange with black dots on edges. Ventrals: 136–158. Subcaudals: 40–56. **DISTRIBUTION** Catanduanes, Luzon, Marinduque, Polillo. **HABITS AND HABITAT** Terrestrial and diurnal. Usually found under rocks of dry river or stream beds in primary and secondary forests.

Luzon Shrub Snake

■ *Oxyrhabdium leporinum leporinum* SVL 610mm; TL 714 mm

Adult

Adult

DESCRIPTION Semifossorial snake with pointed snout. Head slightly distinct from neck. Dorsum uniform iridescent reddish-brown to dark grey without markings. Eyes moderate in size and with vertical pupils. No preocular, one long loreal, in contact with second upper labial, and 1–2 postoculars. Upper labials: seven, fourth and fifth (if two postoculars) or fourth–sixth (if one postocular) in contact with eye, lower labials: 6–7. Labials and throat pale yellow. Ventral dirty-white or pale yellow with grey edges. Ventrals: 162–176 (males), 158–184 (females). Subcaudals: 37–57 (males), 33–46 (females). Tail to TL ratio 19–28 per cent (males), 15–20 per cent (females). Hatchlings and juveniles white with distinct broad white nuchal collar and narrow cross-bands on dorsum that fade with age. **DISTRIBUTION** Calayan, Lubang, Luzon, Marinduque, Mindoro. **HABITS AND HABITAT** Semifossorial and nocturnal. Inhabits primary and secondary forests from sea level to 2,000m asl. Usually hides under logs or rocks, or fern and tree roots. Occasionally seen on forest trails and in man-made canals. Predates on earthworms.

Juvenile

Visayan Shrub Snake ■ *Oxyrhabdium leporinum visayanum*

SVL 612 mm; TL 720mm

DESCRIPTION Dorsum dark greyish-brown, with or without nuchal collar and 35–38 light cross-bands on body. Head slightly distinct from neck. Eyes moderate in size and with vertical pupils. No preocular, one long loreal, in contact with second upper labial, and two postoculars. Upper labials: seven, fourth and fifth in contact with eye, lower labials: 6–7. Dorsal scales smooth and 15 scale rows at mid-body. Ventral colour dirty-white. Ventrals: 169–178 (males), 173–177 (females). Subcaudals: 56–65 (males), 48–53 (females). Anal plate single. Tail to TL ratio: 15 per cent (females), 19 per cent (males). **DISTRIBUTION** Cebu, Negros, Panay. **HABITS AND HABITAT** Semifossorial and nocturnal. Inhabits primary and secondary forests from sea level to 1,400m asl. Usually hides under logs or rocks, or fern and tree roots. Predates on earthworms.

Juvenile

Mindanao Shrub Snake

■ *Oxyrhabdium modestum*
SVL 521mm; TL 616mm

DESCRIPTION Dorsum reddish-brown, but lighter on lateral of body. Loreal scale may or may not be in contact with second upper labial. Eyes moderate in size with vertical pupils. Labials and ventral pale yellow. No preocular, one long loreal, and 1–2 postoculars. Upper labials: eight, fifth and sixth in contact with eye. Dorsal scales smooth and 15 scale rows at midbody. Ventrals: 168–187 (males), 162–191 (females). Subcaudals: 60–70 (males), 49–64 (females). Anal plate single. Tail to TL ratio: 20–30 per cent. Males have longer tails than females. Hatchlings and juveniles have distinct broad white nuchal collar that fades with age. **DISTRIBUTION** Basilan, Biliran, Bohol, Camiguin Sur, Dinagat, Leyte, Maripipi, Mindanao, Samar. **HABITS AND HABITAT** Semifossorial and nocturnal. Inhabits forests from sea level to 1,920m asl. Known to predate only on earthworms.

Adult

Schneider's Dog-faced Water Snake

▪ *Cerberus schneiderii* SVL 830mm; TL 1,000mm

DESCRIPTION Aquatic snake with small head and eyes. Head distinct from neck. Dorsum light brown to greenish-grey with dark spots or bars. Eyes small with vertical pupil; 1–2 preoculars, 1 2 postoculars and one loreal. Upper labials: 9–11, none in contact with eye, lower labials: 11–14. Dorsal scales strongly keeled and 21–25 scale rows at mid-body. Ventral dirty-white, pale yellow or light grey with dark markings. Ventrals: 140–165. Subcaudals: 140–165. Anal plate divided. Tail to TL ratio: 19.5 per cent (males), 17 per cent (females).

DISTRIBUTION Bantayan, Bohol, Catanduanes, Cebu, Cuyo, Dinagat, Guinahoan, Jolo, Lahuy, Luzon, Masbate, Mindanao, Negros, Palawan, Panay, Polillo, Romblon, Sabitang-Laya, Siargao, Siquijor. **HABITS AND HABITAT** Aquatic and nocturnal. Inhabits sea water, brackish water and fresh water at sea level to 800m asl. Mainly predates on gobies and occasionally on frogs and crabs. Females give birth to 8–26 young per clutch. New borns 175–250mm TL.

> **PSEUDASPIDIDAE (MOCK SNAKE, KEELED SNAKE & MOCK VIPERS)**
> This small snake family has three genera and a disjunct distribution. Two monotypic genera (*Pseudaspis* and *Pythonodipsas*) occur in sub-Saharan Africa and one genus (*Psammodynastes*) in Southeast Asia.

Common Mock Viper ■ *Psammodynastes pulverulentus*
SVL 480mm; TL 600mm

DESCRIPTION Small snake with cylindrical body and various colour morphs, such as light brown, reddish-brown and grey. Head elongated and distinct from neck. Eyes large with vertical pupils. Large supraocular extends beyond eye, giving fierce-looking appearance; 1–2 preoculars, 1–3 postoculars, 1–2 loreals, and 2+2 or 1+2 temporals. Upper labials: 7–8, third to fifth in contact with eye, lower labials: 7–8. Ventral dirty-white, pale yellow or reddish-brown. Ventrals: 147–178. Subcaudals: 48–66. Tail to TL ratio: 20–23.5 per cent (males), 18–19 per cent (females). **DISTRIBUTION** Balabac, Basilan, Batan, Bohol, Bongao, Busuanga, Camiguin Sur, Cebu, Dinagat, Jolo, Leyte, Luzon, Mindanao, Negros, Palawan, Panay, Polillo, Sabtang, Samar, Siargao. **HABITS AND HABITAT** Terrestrial and diurnal. Mainly predates on small lizards, but also frogs and snakes (Luzon Keelback Snake, p. 128, on Luzon). Females give birth to 3–10 young. Neonates 148–178mm TL.

Mindanao (south-west)

Luzon (south)

Palawan

Mindanao

Negros

> ## Pareidae (Snake-eating Snakes)
> Occurring mainly in Southeast Asia, these snakes are active and primarily predate on snails and slugs. The snail-eating members have asymmetrical lower jaws to extract the soft bodies of snails from their spiral shells. Only one species is represented in the Philippines.

Blunthead Slug Snake ▪ *Aplopeltura boa* SVL 528mm; TL 800mm

DESCRIPTION Small, slender snake with compressed body. Head distinctly blunt. Eyes large with round pupils. Dorsum light brown to dark greyish-brown with blotches. Upper labials have white spots; 8–10 upper labials, not in contact with eye. Dorsal scales smooth and 13 scale rows at mid-body. Ventral scales weakly keeled. Ventrals: 161–173. Subcaudals: 112–131. Anal plate single. Tail long, about a third of TL. **DISTRIBUTION**

Tawi-Tawi

Balabac, Basilan, Luzon (Sorsogon), Mindanao, Palawan, Tawi-Tawi. **HABITS AND HABITAT** Arboreal and nocturnal. Inhabits forests at low elevation and usually seen on shrubs while hunting for prey. Mainly predates on snails and occasionally on lizards. Defence behaviour: mimics a twig by straightening anterior body part and becoming rigid when disturbed. **NOTE** Only recently reported on Luzon in Sorsogon Province, Bicol Peninsula.

Luzon (south)

> ### PYTHONIDAE (PYTHONS)
> Members of the python family have muscular bodies and recurved teeth, and predate on warm-bodied animals. Pythons are usually the largest/longest snake species where they occur. All pythons are oviparous.

Reticulated Python ▪ *Malayopython reticulatus reticulatus*
SVL 6,160mm; TL 7,000mm

DESCRIPTION Very large snake with cylindrical body. Head depressed and distinct from neck. Snout rounded and with heat-sensing pits on labials. Eyes moderate in size with vertical pupils. Postocular black stripe to temple. Dorsum iridescent yellowish-brown with continuous black zigzag line encircling irregular greyish-brown spots. Lateral body has series of white horizontal bars with black borders. Ventral dirty-white. **DISTRIBUTION** Apulit, Basilan, Bohol, Bongao, Cagayan, Calauit, Calicoan, Catanduanes, Cebu, Dalupiri, Guimaras, Itbayat, Jolo, Lagen, Leyte, Lubang, Luzon, Marinduque, Masbate, Mindanao, Mindoro, Miniloc, Negros, Palawan, Panay, Pangulasian, Polillo, Samar, Siargao, Siasi, Sibutu, Siquijor, Tablas, Tawi-Tawi. **HABITS AND HABITAT** Nocturnal, and both terrestrial and arboreal. Often seen near waterbodies. Predates on mammals (wild boar, deer, monkeys, rats, bats), birds (jungle fowl, hornbills), and reptiles including the Panay

Forest and Palawan Water Monitor Lizards (pp. 75 and 82). Females usually lay 11–46 eggs per clutch but larger clutches of >100 eggs have been reported. Egg incubation 75–90 days. Hatchlings 680–780mm TL. **NOTE** One of the biggest extant snakes in the world with reported maximum TL of 10m on Sulawesi Island, Indonesia. Large individuals increasingly rare, with no verified report of more than 7m length in the Philippines. Due to large size and strength, capable of constricting adult humans. Although non-venomous, its sharp teeth can cause serious injuries.

TYPHLOPIDAE (WORM SNAKES)
Also known as blind snakes, worm snakes are characterized by their small body size, smooth dorsal scales and burrowing habit. They generally feed on larvae of insects and small earthworms. Both asexual and sexual reproduction methods are known in the Typhlopidae family.

Brahminy Worm Snake ▪ *Indotyphlops braminus* SVL 176mm; TL 180mm

DESCRIPTION All-female snake than can reproduce through parthenogenesis. Often mistaken for earthworm due to similar colour, size and habitat. Eyes small. Two nasal scales; superior scale significantly larger than inferior scale. Snout rounded and lighter coloured. Four upper labial scales, not in contact with eye. Preocular in contact with second and third upper labials. Dorsum uniform light reddish-brown to black. Dorsal scales smooth and 20 scale rows at mid-body. Short tail ends in spine. **DISTRIBUTION** Agutayan, Apo, Barit, Basilan, Batan, Bantayan, Bohol, Boracay, Busuanga, Calauit, Camiguin Norte, Camiguin Sur, Catanduanes, Cebu, Dalupiri, Gigantes Sur, Guimaras, Ibahos, Jolo, Luzon, Mactan, Marinduque, Masbate, Mindanao, Maybag, Mindoro, Negros, Pacijan, Palawan, Pamilacan, Panay, Ponson, Panubolon, Polillo, Samar, Semirara, Sibay, Sibuyan, Tintiman. **HABITS AND HABITAT** Introduced in many parts of the world including the Philippines. Fossorial snake commonly seen under pots, in compost piles and in rocks in gardens and other disturbed areas from sea level to 2,000m asl. Females reproduce without fertilization and lay 1–7 eggs per clutch, each the size of a rice grain. Feeds on small earthworms, and insect eggs and larvae.

Cebu Worm Snake ■ *Malayotyphlops hypogius* SVL 338mm

DESCRIPTION Small fossorial snake with cylindrical body and rounded snout. Dorsum uniform dark brown. Ventral reddish-brown. Preocular in contact with second and third upper labials (v third only in the following Philippine snakes: **Canlaon Worm Snake** M. *canlaonensis*, **Red Worm Snake** M. *rubra* and **Red-tailed Worm Snake** M. *ruficauda*). Third upper labial extends dorsally to level of nostril. Dorsal scales smooth and 24 scale rows at mid-body (v 26 in M. *rubra*, 30 in M. *canlaonensis* and M. *ruficauda*). **DISTRIBUTION** Cebu. **HABITS AND HABITAT** Fossorial snake usually seen under rotting leaf litter in secondary forests. Information on biology limited.

Cuming's Worm Snake ■ *Ramphotyphlops cumingii* SVL 342mm

DESCRIPTION Uniform light reddish-brown with cylindrical body. Preocular narrower than ocular and nasal scale, and in contact with third upper labial. Four upper labial scales; third overlaps ocular scale. Dorsal scale smooth and 24–28 scale rows at mid-body. **DISTRIBUTION** Bohol, Cebu, Marinduque, Masbate, Mindanao, Negros, Panay, Polillo, Sibuyan, Sicogon. **HABITS AND HABITAT** Has been seen climbing on twigs. Little information available on biology. **NOTE** Uncertain taxonomy and distribution.

Xenopeltidae (Sunbeam Snakes)

This is a monotypic family with two recognized species occurring across Asia. Dorsal scales are iridescent and smooth.

Sunbeam Snake ■ *Xenopeltis unicolor* SVL 292mm; TL 350mm

DESCRIPTION Head wedge shaped, flat and not distinct from neck. Snout rounded. Eyes very small. One large preocular; loreal absent. Eight upper and lower labials. First upper labial in contact with internasal. Dorsum iridescent, uniform purplish-brown with smooth scales. Scale rows at mid-body: 15. Ventrals white. Juveniles have broad white collar that fades with age. **DISTRIBUTION** Balabac, Bongao, Jolo, Palawan, Sanga-Sanga. **HABITS AND HABITAT** Semi-fossorial and nocturnal. Secretive snake that moves slowly. Often seen after rain. Feeds on frogs, lizards and snakes. Females lay 6–17 eggs per clutch.

ELAPIDAE (ELAPIDS)
Venomous snakes belonging to the elapid family are spread across the region, and include cobras, king cobras, coral snakes and kraits. Terrestrial elapids are mainly diurnal and often encountered in agricultural areas and near human habitats. Elapid snakebites are harmful to humans and cause many hospitalizations, long-term disabilities and deaths each year, especially in agricultural workers and residents in rural areas. Sea kraits (subfamily Laticaudinae) and sea snakes (subfamily Hydrophiinae) are docile but highly venomous.

Turtle-headed Sea Snake ▪ *Emydocephalus annulatus* TL 750mm

DESCRIPTION Moderate-sized sea snake. Head scales large and irregular. Rostral scale has conical projection. Three enlarged upper labial scales. Dorsum variable from banded to uniform black, dark grey or dark brown. Alternating black and creamy-white to yellowish on banded individuals. Black cross-bands wider than light cross-bands, which may be

immaculate or with black spots. Dorsal scale rows at mid-body: 15–17. Ventrals: 125–145. Subcaudals: 20–40. No maxillary teeth present following very small fangs. **DISTRIBUTION** Apo, Bohol, Mindanao, Negros, Siquijor; Snake Reef near Pamilacan, Cang-alwang Reef near Siquijor. **HABITS AND HABITAT** Strictly marine and usually seen in shallow reefs at 3–40m depth. Feeds on demersal fish eggs. Females give birth to live young. VENOMOUS

Stokes' Sea Snake
▪ *Hydrophis stokesii* TL 1,600mm

DESCRIPTION Body exceptionally thick. Large head, varying from black, olive to yellowish. Dorsum light brown to yellowish with dark brown cross-bands or bars. Scales strongly imbricate, pointed, keeled or with tubercles. Body scales on neck: 37–47, around body: 46–63. Ventrals: 226–286. Maxillary teeth following fangs: 6–7 **DISTRIBUTION** Gigantes Sur, Boracay. **HABITS AND HABITAT** Strictly marine species. VENOMOUS

Yellow-lipped Sea Krait ■ *Laticauda colubrina* SVL 1,208mm; TL 1,420mm

DESCRIPTION Uniform light or dark grey with narrower black transverse bands than lighter interspaces. Snout, upper lip and upper temporal pale yellow. Dorsal scales smooth, and 21–25 scale rows at mid-body. Ventral scales pale yellow and large, one-third to one-half width of body. Tail paddle shaped to aid in swimming. **DISTRIBUTION** Babuyan Claro, Barit, Calayan, Sabitang-Laya, Lahuy, Lahos, Dalupiri, Mabag, Bantayan, Bohol,

Cebu, Jolo, Luzon, Mindanao, Negros, Panay, Siquijor, Sitangki. **HABITS AND HABITAT** Diurnal and aquatic. Inhabits coral reefs and predates on small eels. Capable of diving up to 60m in search of food. Frequents rock outcrops near shores and rocky islets. Marine, but comes on to land to digest food, shed its skin, breed and lay eggs. Females lay 4–20 eggs per clutch. Limited information on Philippine populations due to lack of studies. VENOMOUS

Blue-lipped Sea Krait

■ *Laticauda laticaudata*
SVL 960mm; TL 1,070mm

DESCRIPTION Dorsal bluish-grey. Broad black transverse bands about equal in size to lighter interspaces throughout body and tail. Snout and upper lip bluish-grey, and 19 scale rows at mid-body. Ventral scales large, one-third to one-half width of body. Tail paddle shaped to aid in swimming. **DISTRIBUTION** Bantayan, Calayan, Gato, Jolo, Luzon, Mindanao, Mindoro, Samar. **HABITS AND HABITAT** Diurnal and aquatic. Inhabits coral reefs and feeds mainly on small eels. Also found on small, rocky islands hiding under rocks or in crevices. Very limited information on Philippine populations due to lack of studies. VENOMOUS

Two-lined Coral Snake ■ *Calliophis bilineatus* SVL 663mm; TL 717mm

DESCRIPTION Dorsum dark brown with pair of cream or yellow dorsolateral stripes. Head not distinct from neck, snout orange and rounded, and upper lip cream. Ventral cream with 2–3 dark brown cross-bars that are not in contact with edges of dorsal scales. Tail short and subcaudal bright orange. **DISTRIBUTION** Balabac, Busuanga, Calauit, Culion, Lagen, Palawan. **HABITS AND HABITAT** Nocturnal and terrestrial. Usually seen slithering on forest floors or hiding in leaf litter. Twists and turns to exhibit bright subcaudal when threatened. Documented predating on conspecific on Palawan Island. VENOMOUS

Ventral

Dorsal

Defensive behaviour

Philippine Coral Snake ■ *Calliophis philippinus*
SVL 652mm; TL 713mm **e**

DESCRIPTION Dorsum dark brown with pair of brown dorsolateral stripes. Head not distinct from neck, and snout rounded. Ventrals cream with two-scale-wide cross-bars that are in contact with edges of dorsal scales. Hatchlings/juveniles (illustrated) dark brown with regular spaced white bars on body sides and discontiguous orange bars on vertebrals (2–4 scales); fade with age. Tail short and subcaudals bright reddish-orange. **DISTRIBUTION** Camiguin Sur, Dinagat, Mindanao, Samar. **HABITS AND HABITAT** Nocturnal and terrestrial. Inhabits primary forests to disturbed habitats. Usually found under logs and leaf litter. Exposes bright reddish-orange subcaudal when threatened. VENOMOUS

Dinagat Banded Coral Snake ■ *Calliophis salitan*
SVL 856mm; TL 997mm

DESCRIPTION Large-bodied coral snake with bright reddish-orange tail. Dorsal head black; eyes round and small. Upper labials: six, lower labials: seven. Posterior upper lip and throat off-white. Dorsum has nine broad bands between pale yellowish-brown interspaces. Dorsal scales smooth, and 13 scale rows along entire body. Ventrals off-white with broad black cross-bars. Tail to TL ratio 14.1 per cent; subcaudals divided. **DISTRIBUTION** Dinagat, Mindanao. **HABITS AND HABITAT** Nocturnal and terrestrial. Holotype was seen on bank of forest stream at 195m asl. Known only from three individuals. VENOMOUS

Luzon Barred Coral Snake ■ *Hemibungarus calligaster*
SVL 495mm; TL 525mm ⓔ

DESCRIPTION Dorsum uniform black with 44–75 narrow white transverse bands. Head not distinct from neck. Snout rounded and orange. Two preoculars, loreal absent. Upper labials: six, lower labials: seven. Ventrals orange with broad (2–3 scale-wide) transverse

black bands. Tail short and ends with sharp tip. Dorsum of juveniles has alternating, five scales wide black and orange bands. **DISTRIBUTION** Luzon, Mindoro. **HABITS AND HABITAT** Nocturnal and terrestrial. Inhabits primary forests to disturbed areas. Feeds on small snakes such as Gervais' Dwarf Snake (p. 96). Twists and turns to show bright orange underside when threatened. VENOMOUS

Juvenile

Adult

McClung's Barred Coral Snake

■ *Hemibungarus mcclungi* SVL 270mm; TL 293mm

DESCRIPTION Dorsum uniform black with narrow transverse white bands. One preocular, two postoculars, loreal absent. Upper labials: six, third and fourth in contact with eye, lower labials: six. Dorsal scales smooth; 15 scale rows at mid-body. Ventral bright orange with broad black bands divided by narrow white band. Short tail ends in sharp point. Dorsum of juveniles alternating black (6–8 scales wide) and pale orange (4–5 scales wide). Temporal region white or light orange. **DISTRIBUTION** Catanduanes, Luzon, Polillo. **HABITS AND HABITAT** Nocturnal and terrestrial. Occurs in primary forests to disturbed areas. Biology little known, but probably similar in habits to the Luzon Barred Coral Snake (opposite). VENOMOUS

Juvenile

Adult

Northern Philippine Cobra ■ *Naja philippinensis*
SVL 1,220mm; TL 1,410mm **e**

DESCRIPTION Dorsal uniform light brown to dark grey with smooth scales. One preocular, three postoculars, loreal absent. Upper labials: seven, third and fourth in contact with eye, lower labials: eight; 21–23 scale rows at mid-body. Ventral scales light brown or pale yellow. Juveniles: head olive; nape olive with irregular-shaped dark markings; dorsal body and tail dark brown to black with extensive light yellowish reticulated pattern.

Ventral *Dorsal*

DISTRIBUTION Calayan, Catanduanes, Lubang, Luzon, Marinduque, Masbate, Mindoro. **HABITS AND HABITAT** Diurnal and terrestrial. Inhabits primary forests, but common in agricultural areas from sea level to >1,000m asl, where it predates on rodents and frogs, including poisonous Marine Toad *Rhinella marina*. Capable of spraying venom through its short fangs. VENOMOUS

Hatchling

Southern Philippine Cobra ■ *Naja samarensis*
SVL 921mm; TL 1,080mm

DESCRIPTION Dorsal black with smooth scales. Interstitial skin yellow, making net-like pattern when body is distended. One preocular, three postoculars, loreal absent. Upper labials: seven, lower labials: eight; 19 scale rows at mid-body. Throat and first few ventral scales yellow followed by dark grey ventrals. **DISTRIBUTION** Basilan, Bohol, Camiguin Sur, Leyte, Mindanao, Samar, Siquijor. **HABITS AND HABITAT** Diurnal and terrestrial. Occurs in primary forests to agricultural areas at sea level to 1,100m asl. Mainly predates on rodents, as well as snakes and frogs, including poisonous Marine Toad *Rhinella marina*. Capable of spraying venom through its short fangs. VENOMOUS

Palawan Spitting Cobra

■ *Naja sumatrana miolepis* SVL 1,230mm; TL 1,400mm

DESCRIPTION Dorsal uniform dark grey to black, with or without 'V'-shaped marking on nape. Dorsal scales smooth. Lateral of face light brown. One preocular, three postoculars, loreal absent. Upper labials: seven, lower labials: eight (fourth inverted triangle shaped and smallest; between third and fifth); 19 scale rows at mid-body. Neck and first few ventrals light brown with faint dark markings, followed by grey ventrals. Juveniles: dorsal black with light yellowish-brown marking on nape and up to 11 light transverse bands on body and tail; lateral face yellowish-brown. **DISTRIBUTION** Busuanga, Calauit, Culion, Palawan, Pangulasian. **HABITS AND HABITAT** Diurnal and terrestrial. Occurs in primary forests, but more commonly seen in disturbed areas. Mainly predates on rodents. Capable of spraying venom through its short fangs. VENOMOUS

King Cobra ▪ *Ophiophagus hannah* SVL 3,400mm; TL 4,250mm

DESCRIPTION The most iconic of all venomous snakes in the world. Species complex. Dorsal highly variable, from brown and olive, to black. Large pair of occipital scales diagnostic. One preocular, three postoculars, loreal absent. Upper labials: seven, third and fourth in contact with eye, lower labials: eight. Dorsal scales smooth, with or without black edges, and 15 scale rows at mid-body. Ventrals light brown or pale yellow. Posterior body and tail of light-coloured individuals have dark, net-like pattern. Juveniles black with numerous contiguous or broken transverse narrow bands on dorsal body and tail.
DISTRIBUTION Alabat, Balabac, Bohol, Bongao, Busuanga, Catanduanes, Cebu, Culion, Dinagat, Guimaras, Jolo, Leyte, Lubang, Luzon, Marinduque, Mindanao, Mindoro, Miniloc, Negros, North Guntao, Palawan, Panay, Pangulasian, Polillo, Romblon, Samar, Semirara, Tandubas. **HABITS AND HABITAT** Diurnal and terrestrial. Occurs in primary forests to forest edges adjacent to disturbed areas. Usually seen near waterbodies such as forest streams, rivers and mangroves. Predates on snakes, as well as on water monitor lizards. Seasonal breeder; males engage in ritual combat to establish dominance. At 2–3 weeks before egg laying, female constructs nest by gathering dried leaves. Females exhibit parental care by guarding eggs and repairing nests. **NOTE** Recent phylogenetic study concluded that King Cobra on Luzon island is distinct species. VENOMOUS

Palawan

Luzon

> **VIPERIDAE (VIPERS)**
> Snakes in the viper family have a pair of relatively long fangs, which can be folded on the roof of the mouth. The large, triangular head, vertical pupils and extended supraocular scales make them look fierce. Vipers are sit-and-wait predators that stay still in one location for a long time but are able to strike quickly to catch prey or when threatened.

Philippine Yellow-spotted Pitviper

■ *Trimeresurus flavomaculatus* SVL 1,040mm; TL 1,200mm

DESCRIPTION Species complex with various colour and pattern morphs. Typical dorsal colour green with grey tail-tip. Ventral yellowish-green without markings. Head distinct from neck, eye round, pupil vertical, and iris light to dark orange. Scales on chin (gular) smooth. Three elongated preoculars. Facial pit in contact with centre and lower preoculars and posterior of second upper labial. Dorsal scales bordering ventrals yellow or white.
DISTRIBUTION Babuyan Claro, Biliran, Bohol, Calayan, Camiguin Norte, Camiguin Sur, Catanduanes, Dalipiri, Dinagat, Jolo, Leyte, Luzon, Mindanao, Mindoro, Negros, Panay, Polillo, Siquijor. **HABITS AND HABITAT** Sit-and-wait predator often seen on small trees and stream banks in primary to secondary forests at sea level to 700m asl. Predates on fish, frogs, lizards and rodents. Females lay up to 20 eggs per clutch and exhibit parental care by guarding eggs. VENOMOUS

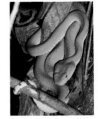

Mindanao

Mindanao

Luzon

Luzon

Luzon

McGregor's Pitviper ■ *Trimeresurus mcgregori* SVL 745mm; TL 865mm

DESCRIPTION Polymorphic species ranging from white, yellow and reddish-brown, to grey with or without irregular dark markings. Head triangular from above and distinct from neck. Eyes round with vertical pupils and white to light brown irises. Upper labials: 10, first small, triangular and in contact with rostral, lower labials: 11. Scale rows at mid-body: 21. Facial pit below preocular and between second and third upper labial. Tail prehensile. **DISTRIBUTION** Batan, Calayan, Camiguin Norte. **HABITS AND HABITAT** Sit-and-wait predator often seen in riparian habitats. Occurs in forests and disturbed habitats. Females exhibit parental care by guarding eggs. Illegal collection for domestic and international pet trade ongoing. VENOMOUS

White (female)

Red

Yellow with dark markings

Banded Keel-throated Pitviper

■ *Tropidolaemus subannulatus* SVL 850mm; TL 1,000mm

DESCRIPTION Species complex with colour ranging from green to yellowish-green. Dorsum has red and white spots (males), or white and blue, or white and red vertical stripes (females). Head broad at base, eyes moderate with vertical pupils, and irises orange to dark reddish-orange. White and blue, or white and red stripes from snout to temple. Upper labials: 10–11, lower labials: 12. Scales on head and chin strongly keeled. Scales on dorsum keeled. Scale rows at mid-body: 21–23 (males), 21–29 (females). Ventrals lighter yellowish-green. Tail prehensile and colour distinct from body, ranging from grey, to pale yellowish-orange. **DISTRIBUTION** Balabac, Basilan, Bohol, Calicoan, Cebu, Dinagat, Jolo, Lagen, Leyte, Luzon, Mindanao, Miniloc, Negros, Palawan, Panay, Samar, Siasi, Sibutu, Tablas, Tumindao. **HABITS AND HABITAT** Arboreal and nocturnal. Inhabits primary and secondary forests near riparian habitats; rarely in agricultural areas. Usually seen resting on small trees by day, but occasionally on branches 6m above the ground. Females give birth to live young. VENOMOUS

Palawan

Mindanao

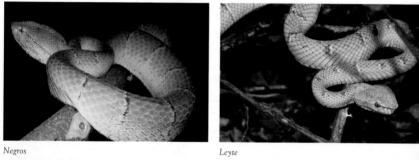

Negros

Leyte

Mindanao

Luzon

Schultze's Pitviper ▪ *Trimeresurus schultzei*
SVL 1,020mm; TL 1,220mm (e)

DESCRIPTION Dorsal scales on head and body green with black margins, forming extensive net-like pattern. Dorsal scales keeled. Head distinct from neck, eyes round, pupils vertical, irises light brown or orange, and upper lip yellow. Dorsal scale rows at mid-body: 21. Dorsal scales bordering ventrals yellow, forming distinct line. Ventrals greenish-yellow with light blue edges. Tail red with longitudinal white stripe on each side. **DISTRIBUTION** Balabac, Palawan. **HABITS AND HABITAT** Sit-and-wait predator often seen in riparian habitats in primary and secondary forests at sea level to 700m asl. VENOMOUS

Southern Philippine Keel-throated Pitviper
▪ *Tropidolaemus philippensis* SVL 390mm; TL 455mm (e)

DESCRIPTION Dorsal turquoise-green (males) or pale green (females), with black net-like pattern. Head broad at base, triangular and distinct from neck. Scales on head and body keeled, pupil vertical, iris white to dark orange. Upper labials: 15–16, lower labials: 16–17. Black postocular stripe. Ventrals pale green. Population in Zamboanga Peninsula and Basilan may be distinct species. **DISTRIBUTION** Dinagat, Leyte, Mindanao, Samar. **HABITS AND HABITAT** Arboreal and nocturnal. Usually found on branches of small trees adjacent to riparian habitats. VENOMOUS

Distributional Status
Endemic (E)
Native (N)
Introduced (I)

IUCN Red List of Threatened Species (version 2022-2)
Critically Endangered (CR) Species that meet any of the categories and corresponding criteria A–E for CR and are considered to face an extremely high risk of extinction in the wild.
Endangered (EN) Species that meet any of the categories and corresponding criteria A–E for EN and are considered to face a very high risk of extinction in the wild.
Vulnerable (VU) Species that meet any of the categories and corresponding criteria A–E for VU and are considered to face a high risk of extinction in the wild.
Near Threatened (NT) Species that do not qualify for the categories and corresponding criteria A–E for CR, EN or VU, but are close to or expected to meet them in the near future.
Least Concern (LC) Species that do not qualify for the categories and corresponding criteria A–E for CR, EN or VU. Species that are not facing significant threats, very abundant or widely distributed are included in this category.
Data Deficient (DD) Species that do not have sufficient information to make a direct or indirect extinction risk assessment.
Not Evaluated (NE) Species that are not evaluated for extinction risk.

Philippine Red List DAO 2019-09
Critically Endangered (CR) Species that are facing extremely high risk of extinction in the wild in the immediate future.
Endangered (EN) Species that are not CR, but survival in the wild is unlikely if the causal factors continue to operate.
Vulnerable (VU) Species that are neither CR nor EN, but are under threat from adverse factors throughout their range and are likely to be moved to the endangered category in the future.
Other Threatened Species (OTS) Species that are not CR, EN or VU, but are under threat from adverse factors.
Other Wildlife Species (OWS) All species that do not belong to the CR, EN, VU or OTS category.

CITES Appendix
Appendix I lists species that are the most endangered among CITES-listed animals and plants (see Article II, paragraph 1 of the Convention). They are threatened with extinction and CITES prohibits international trade in specimens of these species except when the purpose of the import is not commercial (see Article III), for instance for scientific research. In these exceptional cases, trade may take place provided it is authorized by the granting of both an import permit and an export permit (or re-export

certificate). Article VII of the Convention provides for a number of exemptions to this general prohibition.

Appendix II lists species that are not necessarily now threatened with extinction but that may become so unless trade is closely controlled. It also includes so-called 'look-alike species', that is species whose specimens in trade look like those of species listed for conservation reasons (see Article II, paragraph 2 of the Convention). International trade in specimens of Appendix II species may be authorized by the granting of an export permit or re-export certificate. No import permit is necessary for these species under CITES (although a permit is needed in some countries that have taken stricter measures than CITES requires). Permits or certificates should only be granted if the relevant authorities are satisfied that certain conditions are met, above all that trade will not be detrimental to the survival of the species in the wild. (See Article IV of the Convention).

Appendix III is a list of species included at the request of a Party that already regulates trade in the species and that needs the cooperation of other countries to prevent unsustainable or illegal exploitation (see Article II, paragraph 3, of the Convention). International trade in specimens of species listed in this Appendix is allowed only on presentation of the appropriate permits or certificates. (See Article V of the Convention). **Not Listed** (NL).

English Name	Scientific Name	Luzon	West Visayas	Mindanao	Palawan	Sulu	Sub-faunal Region**	DISTRIBUTIONAL STATUS	PH RED LIST DAO 2019-09	IUCN RED LIST 2022-2	CITES
Crocodylidae (Crocodiles)											
Philippine Crocodile	*Crocodylus mindorensis*	*		*				E	CR	CR	I
Saltwater Crocodile	*Crocodylus porosus*	*		*	*	*		N	CR	LC	I/II~
Agamidae (Agamids)											
Green Crested Lizard	*Bronchocela cristatella*	*	*	*	*			N	OTS	LC	NL
Marbled Crested Lizard	*Bronchocela marmorata*	*						E	OTS	LC	NL
Common Garden Lizard	*Calotes versicolor*	*						I	OWS	LC	NL
Two-spotted Flying Lizard	*Draco bimaculatus*			*		*		E	OWS	LC	NL
Green Flying Lizard	*Draco cyanopterus*			*				E	OWS	LC	NL
Günther's Flying Lizard	*Draco guentheri*			*		*		E	OWS	LC	NL
Jareck's Flying Lizard	*Draco jareckii*						*	E	OWS	LC	NL
Mindanao Flying Lizard	*Draco mindanensis*			*				E	OWS	NT	NL
Ornate Flying Lizard	*Draco ornatus*			*				E	OWS	LC	NL
Palawan Flying Lizard	*Draco palawanensis*				*			E	OWS	LC	NL
Quadras' Flying Lizard	*Draco quadrasi*						*	E	OWS	LC	NL
Reticulated Flying Lizard	*Draco reticulatus*			*			*	E	OWS	LC	NL
Luzon Flying Lizard	*Draco spilopterus*	*	*				*	E	OWS	LC	NL
Mindoro Anglehead Lizard	*Gonocephalus interruptus*							E	OTS	LC	NL
White-spotted Anglehead Lizard	*Gonocephalus semperi*							E	OTS	LC	NL
Negros Anglehead Lizard	*Gonocephalus sophiae*							E	OTS	LC	NL
Philippine Sailfin Lizard	*Hydrosaurus pustulatus*	*	*	*			*	E	OTS	LC	NL

English Name	Scientific Name	Luzon	West Visayas	Mindanao	Palawan	Sulu	Sub-faunal Region**	DISTRIBUTIONAL STATUS	PH RED LIST DAO 2019-09	IUCN RED LIST 2022-2	CITES
Dibamidae (Legless Lizards)											
White Blind Legless Lizard	*Dibamus leucurus*		*	*	*			N	OWS	LC	NL
New Guinea Legless Lizard	*Dibamus novaeguineae*		*					N	OWS	LC	NL
Gekkonidae (Geckos)											
Agusan Bent-toed Gecko	*Cyrtodactylus agusanensis*			*				E	OWS	LC	NL
Annulated Bent-toed Gecko	*Cyrtodactylus annulatus*		*	*			*	E	OWS	LC	NL
Leyte Bent-toed Gecko	*Cyrtodactylus gubaot*						*	E	OWS	LC	NL
Zamboanga Bent-toed Gecko	*Cyrtodactylus jambangan*			*		*		E	OWS	LC	NL
Mamanwa Bent-toed Gecko	*Cyrtodactylus mamanwa*			*				E	OWS	LC	NL
Philippine Bent-toed Gecko	*Cyrtodactylus philippinicus*	*	*					E	OWS	LC	NL
Palawan Bent-toed Gecko	*Cyrtodactylus redimiculus*				*			E	OWS	NT	NL
Sumuroy's Bent-toed Gecko	*Cyrtodactylus sumuroi*						*	E	OWS	LC	NL
Tau't Bato Bent-toed Gecko	*Cyrtodactylus tautbatorum*				*			E	OWS	LC	NL
Tender-skinned Gecko; Common Four-toed Gecko	*Gehyra mutilata*	*	*	*	*		*	N	OWS	LC	NL
Palawan Gecko	*Gekko athymus*				*			E	OWS	NT	NL
Luzon Karst Gecko	*Gekko carusadensis*	*						E	OWS	DD	NL
Leonardo Co's Gecko	*Gekko coi*						*	E	OWS	LC	NL
Babuyan Claro Gecko	*Gekko crombota*						*	E	OWS	LC	NL
Ernst Keller's Gecko	*Gekko ernstkelleri*		*					E	OWS	LC	NL
Tokay Gecko	*Gekko gecko gecko*	*	*	*	*	*		N	OTS	LC	II
Gigante Island Gecko	*Gekko gigante*		*					E	OWS	VU	NL
Palawan Forest Gecko	*Gekko gulat*				*			E	OWS	DD	NL
Philippine Parachute Gecko	*Gekko intermedium*			*			*	E	OTS	LC	NL
Kikuchi's Gecko	*Gekko kikuchii*	*						N	OWS	LC	NL
Mindoro Narrow-disked Gecko	*Gekko mindorensis*	*	*	*			*	E	OWS	LC	NL
Spotted House Gecko	*Gekko monarchus*				*			N	OWS	LC	NL
Palawan Narrow-disked Gecko	*Gekko palawanensis*				*			E	OWS	NT	NL
Taylor's Gecko	*Gekko porosus*						*	E	OWS	LC	NL
Romblon Gecko	*Gekko romblon*						*	E	OWS	LC	NL
Ross' Calayan Gecko	*Gekko rossi*						*	E	OWS	LC	NL
Brooke's House Gecko	*Hemidactylus brookii*	*						N	OWS	LC	NL
Common House Gecko	*Hemidactylus frenatus*	*	*	*	*	*	*	N	OWS	LC	NL
Flat-tailed House Gecko	*Hemidactylus platyurus*	*	*	*	*	*	*	N	OWS	LC	NL
Stejneger's House Gecko	*Hemidactylus stejnegeri*	*	*	*			*	N	OWS	LC	NL
Philippine Slender Gecko	*Hemiphyllodactylus insularis*		*	*	*		*	E	OWS	DD	NL
Indo-Pacific Slender Gecko	*Hemiphyllodactylus typus*		*	*	*		*	N	OWS	LC	NL
Yellow Smooth-scaled Gecko	*Lepidodactylus aureolineatus*		*	*			*	E	OWS	LC	NL
Babuyan Smooth-scaled Gecko/ Scaly-toed	*Lepidodactylus babuyanensis*						*	E	OWS	NE	NL
Ilocano Smooth-scaled Gecko/ Scaly-toed	*Lepidodactylus bakingibut*	*						E	OWS	NE	NL
Batan Smooth-scaled Gecko	*Lepidodactylus balioburius*						*	E	OWS	LC	NL
Bicol Smooth-scaled/Scaly-toed Gecko	*Lepidodactylus bisakol*						*	E	OWS	NE	NL
Christian's Smooth-scaled Gecko	*Lepidodactylus christiani*		*					E	OWS	LC	NL
Herre's Smooth-scaled Gecko	*Lepidodactylus herrei herrei*		*					E	OWS	LC	NL
Median Smooth-scaled Gecko	*Lepidodactylus herrei medianus*		*	*			*	E	OWS	LC	NL

English Name	Scientific Name	Luzon	West Visayas	Mindanao	Palawan	Sulu	Sub-faunal Region**	DISTRIBUTIONAL STATUS	PH RED LIST DAO 2019-09	IUCN RED LIST 2022-2	CITES
Mindanao Smooth-scaled Gecko	Lepidodactylus labialis			*				E	OWS	DD	NL
Common Smooth-scaled Gecko	Lepidodactylus lugubris	*	*		*			N	OWS	LC	NL
Lubang Smooth-scaled Gecko/Scaly-toed	Lepidodactylus nakahiwalay	*						E	OWS	NE	NL
Flat-tailed Smooth-scaled Gecko	Lepidodactylus planicaudus		*	*			*	E	OWS	LC	NL
Diminutive Gecko	Luperosaurus angliit	*					*	E	OWS	DD	NL
Corfield's Gecko	Luperosaurus corfieldi		*					E	OWS	DD	NL
Cuming's Wolf Gecko	Luperosaurus cumingii	*						E	OWS	DD	NL
Jolo Wolf Gecko	Luperosaurus joloensis			*		*		E	OWS	DD	NL
Hidden Wolf Gecko	Luperosaurus kubli	*						E	OWS	LC	NL
MacGregor's Wolf Gecko	Luperosaurus macgregori						*	E	OWS	NT	NL
Palawan Wolf Gecko	Luperosaurus palawanensis				*			E	OWS	DD	NL
West Visayas False Gecko	Pseudogekko atiorum		*					E	OWS	NE	NL
Short-footed False Gecko	Pseudogekko brevipes			*			*	E	OWS	VU	NL
Zamboanga False Gecko	Pseudogekko chavacano			*				E	OWS	NE	NL
Blue Eye-ringed False Gecko	Pseudogekko compresicorpus	*	*				*	E	OWS	LC	NL
Leyte Diminutive False Gecko	Pseudogekko ditoy						*	E	OWS	DD	NL
Bicol Hollow-dwelling Forest Gecko	Pseudogekko hungkag	*						E	OWS	EN	NL
Romblon False Gecko	Pseudogekko isapa						*	E	OWS	VU	NL
Southern Philippine False Gecko	Pseudogekko pungkaypinit			*			*	E	OWS	LC	NL
Polillo False Gecko	Pseudogekko smaragdinus	*					*	E	OTS	LC	NL
Bicol False Gecko	Pseudogekko sumiklab	*						E	OWS	EN	NL
Scincidae (Skinks)											
Bicol Slender Skink	Brachymeles bicolandia	*						E	OWS	LC	NL
Two-coloured Slender Skink	Brachymeles bicolor	*						E	OWS	LC	NL
Bohol Slender Skink	Brachymeles boholensis			*				E	OWS	LC	NL
Beautiful Slender Skink	Brachymeles bonitae	*					*	E	OWS	LC	NL
Boulenger's Short-legged Skink	Brachymeles boulengeri	*					*	E	OWS	LC	NL
Southern Bicol Slender Skink	Brachymeles brevidactylus	*						E	OWS	LC	NL
Burks' Slender Skink	Brachymeles burksi	*					*	E	OWS	LC	NL
Cebu Slender Skink	Brachymeles cebuensis		*					E	OWS	CR	NL
Catanduanes Slender Skink	Brachymeles cobos						*	E	OWS	LC	NL
Tablas Slender Skink	Brachymeles dalawangdaliri						*	E	OWS	LC	NL
Elera's Slender Skink	Brachymeles elerae	*						E	OWS	LC	NL
Graceful Slender Skink	Brachymeles gracilis		*	*				E	OWS	LC	NL
Mindanao Five-digited Slender Skink	Brachymeles hilong			*				E	OWS	LC	NL
Ilocos Slender Skink	Brachymeles ilocandia	*					*	E	OWS	LC	NL
One-fingered Slender Skink/Aurora Slender Skink	Brachymeles isangdaliri	*						E	OWS	DD	NL
Jessi's Slender Skink	Brachymeles kadwa	*					*	E	OWS	LC	NL
Lapinig Slender Skink	Brachymeles libayani			*				E	OWS	LC	NL
Lubang Slender Skink	Brachymeles ligtas	*						E	OWS	LC	NL
Lukban Loam Swimming Skink	Brachymeles lukbani	*						E	OWS	LC	NL
Bicol Loam Swimming Skink	Brachymeles makusog	*					*	E	OWS	LC	NL
Masbate Slender Skink	Brachymeles mapalanggaon		*					E	OWS	VU	NL
Mindoro Slender Skink	Brachymeles mindorensis						*	E	OWS	LC	NL
Catanduanes Limbless Skink	Brachymeles minimus						*	E	OWS	NT	NL
Caraballo Mountain Loam-swimming Skink	Brachymeles muntingkamay	*						E	OWS	LC	NL

English Name	Scientific Name	Luzon	West Visayas	Mindanao	Palawan	Sulu	Sub-faunal Region**	DISTRIBUTIONAL STATUS	PH RED LIST DAO 2019-09	IUCN RED LIST 2022-2	CITES
Southern Philippine Burrowing Skink	Brachymeles orientalis			*			*	E	OWS	LC	NL
PAEF Slender Skink	Brachymeles paeforum						*	E	OWS	LC	NL
Pathfinder's Slender Skink	Brachymeles pathfinderi			*				E	OWS	LC	NL
Eastern Visayas Slender Skink	Brachymeles samad					*		E	OWS	LC	NL
Samar Slender Skink	Brachymeles samarensis					*		E	OWS	NT	NL
Schadenberg's Slender Skink	Brachymeles schadenbergi			*				E	OWS	LC	NL
Sulu Slender Skink	Brachymeles suluensis			*		*		E	OWS	NE	NL
Mt Talinis Slender Skink	Brachymeles talinis		*				*	E	OWS	LC	NL
Taylor's Slender Skink	Brachymeles taylori		*					E	OWS	LC	NL
Tiboli Slender Skink	Brachymeles tiboliorum			*				E	OWS	DD	NL
Western Visayas Three-digited Slender Skink	Brachymeles tridactylus		*					E	OWS	LC	NL
Tungao's Slender Skink	Brachymeles tungaoi		*					E	OWS	LC	NL
Limbless Slender Skink	Brachymeles vermis				*			E	OWS	EN	NL
Vindum's Slender Skink	Brachymeles vindumi				*			E	OWS	DD	NL
Camiguin Sur Slender Skink	Brachymeles vulcani			*				E	OWS	LC	NL
Northern Luzon Slender Skink	Brachymeles wrighti	*						E	OWS	DD	NL
Palawan Tree Skink	Dasia griffini				*			E	OWS	VU	NL
Gray Tree Skink	Dasia grisea	*					*	N	OWS	LC	NL
Half-banded Tree Skink	Dasia semicincta			*				N	OWS	DD	NL
Mangrove Skink	Emoia atrocostata	*	*	*	*	*	*	N	OWS	LC	NL
Pacific Blue-tailed Skink	Emoia caeruleocauda			*	*	*		N	OWS	LC	NL
Red-tailed Skink	Emoia ruficauda			*				N	OWS	LC	NL
Alcala's Sun Skink	Eutropis alcalai						*	E	OWS	DD	NL
Luzon Montane Sun Skink	Eutropis bontocensis	*						E	OWS	LC	NL
Northern Philippine Sun Skink	Eutropis borealis	*					*	E	OWS	LC	NL
Caraga Sun Skink	Eutropis caraga			*				E	OWS	LC	NL
Luzon Sun Skink	Eutropis cumingi	*					*	E	OWS	LC	NL
Copper Sun Skink	Eutropis cuprea			*				E	OWS	LC	NL
Engle's Sun Skink	Eutropis englei			*				E	OWS	LC	NL
Upland Sun Skink	Eutropis gubataas	*					*	E	OWS	LC	NL
Mindoro Sun Skink	Eutropis indeprensa						*	E	OWS	LC	NL
Striking Philippine Sun Skink	Eutropis islamaliit	*					*	N	OWS	NE	NL
Lapulapu's Sun Skink	Eutropis lapulapu		*	*			*	E	OWS	NE	NL
Many-keeled Sun Skink	Eutropis multicarinata			*			*	E	OWS	LC	NL
Many-lined Sun Skink	Eutropis multifasciata	*	*	*	*			N	OWS	LC	NL
Rough-scaled Skink	Eutropis rudis					*		N	OWS	LC	NL
Palawan Sun Skink	Eutropis sahulinghangganan			*				E	OWS	LC	NL
Sibalom Sun Skink	Eutropis sibalom		*					E	OWS	DD	NL
Negros Forest Skink	Insulasaurus arborens		*					E	OWS	LC	NL
Mt Matalingahan Forest Skink	Insulasaurus traanorum				*			E	OWS	LC	NL
Mt Victoria Forest Skink	Insulasaurus victoria				*			E	OWS	NT	NL
Wright's Forest Skink	Insulasaurus wrighti				*			E	OWS	DD	NL
Philippine Emerald Tree Skink	Lamprolepis smaragdina philippinica	*	*	*	*		*	E	OWS	LC	NL
Bronze Slender Tree Skink	Lipinia auriculata auriculata		*					E	OWS	LC	NL
Herre's Slender Tree Skink	Lipinia auriculata herrei		*				*	E	OWS	LC	NL
Kemp's Slender Tree Skink	Lipinia auriculata kempi						*	E	OWS	LC	NL
Leviton's Slender Tree Skink	Lipinia pulchella levitoni	*						E	OWS	LC	NL
Yellow-striped Slender Tree Skink	Lipinia pulchella pulchella	*		*			*	E	OWS	LC	NL

English Name	Scientific Name	Luzon	West Visayas	Mindanao	Palawan	Sulu	Sub-faunal Region**	DISTRIBUTIONAL STATUS	PH RED LIST DAO 2019-09	IUCN RED LIST 2022-2	CITES
Taylor's Slender Tree Skink	*Lipinia pulchella taylori*		*					E	OWS	LC	NL
Four-striped Slender Tree Skink	*Lipinia quadrivittata*		*	*	*		*	N	OWS	LC	NL
Rabor's Slender Tree Skink	*Lipinia rabori*		*					E	OWS	DD	NL
Semper's Slender Tree Skink	*Lipinia semperi*			*				E	OWS	DD	NL
Striped Slender Tree Skink	*Lipinia subvittata*			*				N	OWS	NT	NL
Vulcan Slender Tree Skink	*Lipinia vulcania*						*	E	OWS	DD	NL
Zamboanga Slender Tree Skink	*Lipinia zamboangensis*						*	E	OWS	DD	NL
Palawan Supple Skink	*Lygosoma tabonorum*				*			E	OWS	LC	NL
Philippine Giant Forest Skink	*Otosaurus cumingi*	*		*				E	OWS	LC	NL
Mt Makiling Dwarf Skink	*Parvoscincus abstrusus*	*					*	E	OWS	NT	NL
Agta Forest Skink	*Parvoscincus agtorum*	*						E	OWS	DD	NL
Diesmos' Forest Skink	*Parvoscincus arvindiesmosi*						*	E	OWS	LC	NL
Aurora Forest Skink	*Parvoscincus aurorus*	*						E	OWS	NE	NL
Mt Banahao Forest Skink	*Parvoscincus banahaoensis*	*						E	OWS	VU	NL
Beyer's Forest Skink	*Parvoscincus beyeri*	*						E	OWS	VU	NL
Boying's Zambales Mountain Skink	*Parvoscincus boyingi*	*						E	OWS	NE	NL
Sierra Madre Mountain Skink	*Parvoscincus decipiens*	*						E	OWS	LC	NL
Cordillera Aquatic Skink	*Parvoscincus duwendorum*	*						E	OWS	NE	NL
Aurora Mountain Skink	*Parvoscincus hadros*	*						E	OWS	DD	NL
Igorot Cordillera Mountain Skink	*Parvoscincus igorotorum*	*						E	OWS	NE	NL
McGuire's Forest Skink	*Parvoscincus jimmymcguirei*	*						E	OWS	LC	NL
Mt Kitanglad Forest Skink	*Parvoscincus kitangladensis*			*				E	OWS	LC	NL
Bicol Forest Skink	*Parvoscincus laterimaculatus*	*						E	OWS	DD	NL
Lawton's Forest Skink	*Parvoscincus lawtoni*	*						E	OWS	DD	NL
White-spotted Forest Skink	*Parvoscincus leucospilos*	*						E	OWS	LC	NL
Northern Luzon Forest Skink	*Parvoscincus luzonensis*	*						E	OWS	NT	NL
Aurora Aquatic Skink	*Parvoscincus manananggalae*	*						E	OWS	NE	NL
Mt Palali Dwarf Skink	*Parvoscincus palaliensis*	*						E	OWS	LC	NL
Palawan Forest Skink	*Parvoscincus palawanensis*				*			E	OWS	VU	NL
Sison's Dwarf Skink	*Parvoscincus sisoni*		*					E	OWS	VU	NL
Steere's Forest Skink	*Parvoscincus steerei*	*	*	*			*	E	OWS	LC	NL
Brown's Forest Skink	*Parvoscincus tagapayo*	*						E	OWS	NT	NL
Sierra Madre Mountain Aquatic Skink	*Parvoscincus tikbalangi*	*						E	OWS	NE	NL
Southern Philippine Giant Forest Skink	*Pinoyscincus abdictus abdictus*			*			*	E	OWS	LC	NL
Northern Philippine Giant Forest Skink	*Pinoyscincus abdictus aquilonius*	*					*	E	OWS	LC	NL
Cox's Giant Forest Skink	*Pinoyscincus coxi coxi*			*			*	E	OWS	LC	NL
Mt Makiling Forest Skink	*Pinoyscincus coxi divergens*	*	*				*	E	OWS	LC	NL
Western Visayas Giant Forest Skink	*Pinoyscincus jagori grandis*		*					E	OWS	LC	NL
Jagor's Forest Skink	*Pinoyscincus jagori jagori*			*			*	E	OWS	LC	NL
Eastern Visayas Forest Skink	*Pinoyscincus llanosi*						*	E	OWS	NT	NL
Mindanao Forest Skink	*Pinoyscincus mindanensis*			*				E	OWS	LC	NL
Pointed-snouted Forest Skink	*Sphenomorphus acutus*			*			*	E	OWS	LC	NL
Fairy Forest Skink	*Sphenomorphus diwata*			*				E	OWS	DD	NL
Banded Forest Skink	*Sphenomorphus fasciatus*			*			*	E	OWS	LC	NL
Variegated Forest Skink	*Sphenomorphus variegatus*			*			*	E	OWS	LC	NL

English Name	Scientific Name	Luzon	West Visayas	Mindanao	Palawan	Sulu	Sub-faunal Region**	DISTRIBUTIONAL STATUS	PH RED LIST DAO 2019-09	IUCN RED LIST 2022-2	CITES
Bowring's Supple Skink	*Subdoluseps bowringii*						*	N	OWS	LC	NL
Davao Keeled Water Skink	*Tropidophorus davaoensis*			*				E	OWS	LC	NL
Philippine Keeled Water Skink	*Tropidophorus grayi*	*	*				*	E	OTS	LC	NL
Misamis Keeled Water Skink	*Tropidophorus misaminius*			*				E	OWS	LC	NL
Partello's Keeled Water Skink	*Tropidophorus partelloi*			*				E	OWS	LC	NL
Zamboanga Forest Skink	*Tytthoscincus atrigularis*			*				E	OWS	LC	NL
Sulu Forest Skink	*Tytthoscincus biparietalis*			*		*		E	OWS	EN	NL
Varanidae (Monitor Lizards)											
Bangon Water Monitor Lizard	*Varanus bangonorum*						*	E	OTS	LC	II
Northern Luzon Forest Monitor Lizard	*Varanus bitatawa*	*						E	VU	NT	II
Mindanao Water Monitor Lizard	*Varanus cumingi*			*				E	OTS	LC	II
Enteng's Water Monitor Lizard	*Varanus dalubhasa*	*					*	E	OTS	LC	II
Panay Forest Monitor Lizard	*Varanus mabitang*		*					E	CR	EN	II
Luzon Water Monitor Lizard	*Varanus marmoratus*	*					*	E	OTS	LC	II
Western Visayas Water Monitor Lizard	*Varanus nuchalis*		*				*	E	OTS	LC	II
Southern Luzon Forest Monitor Lizard	*Varanus olivaceus*	*					*	E	VU	VU	II
Palawan Water Monitor Lizard	*Varanus palawanensis*				*	*		E	OTS	LC	II
Rasmussen's Water Monitor Lizard	*Varanus rasmusseni*					*		E	OTS	LC	II
Samar Water Monitor Lizard	*Varanus samarensis*		*				*	E	OTS	LC	II
Acrochordidae (Wart Snakes)											
Marine File Snake, Wart Snake	*Acrochordus granulatus*	*	*		*			N	OWS	LC	NL
Colubridae (Colubrids)											
Asian Vine Snake	*Ahaetulla prasina prasina*					*		N	OWS	LC	NL
Philippine Vine Snake	*Ahaetulla prasina preocularis*	*	*	*		*	*	E	OWS	LC	NL
Sulu Vine Snake	*Ahaetulla prasina suluensis*					*		E	OWS	LC	NL
Philippine Blunt-headed Cat Snake	*Boiga angulata*	*	*	*			*	E	OTS	LC	NL
Dog-toothed Cat Snake	*Boiga cynodon*	*	*	*		*	*	N	OTS	LC	NL
Luzon Mangrove Snake	*Boiga dendrophila divergens*	*					*	E	OTS	LC	NL
Mindanao Mangrove Snake	*Boiga dendrophila latifasciata*			*			*	E	OTS	LC	NL
Panay Mangrove Snake	*Boiga dendrophila levitoni*		*					E	OTS	LC	NL
Palawan Mangrove Snake	*Boiga dendrophila multicincta*				*			E	OTS	LC	NL
White-spotted Cat Snake	*Boiga drapiezii*			*		*		N	OWS	LC	NL
Philippine Cat Snake	*Boiga philippina*	*					*	E	OTS	LC	NL
Schultze's Blunt-headed Cat Snake	*Boiga schultzei*				*			E	OWS	LC	NL
Alcala's Reed Snake	*Calamaria alcalai*						*	E	OWS	DD	NL
Luzon Reed Snake	*Calamaria bitorques*	*	*					E	OWS	LC	NL
Philippine Reed Snake	*Calamaria gervaisii*		*	*			*	E	OWS	LC	NL
Jolo Reed Snake	*Calamaria joloensis*					*		E	OWS	DD	NL
Variable Reed Snake	*Calamaria lumbricoidea*			*			*	N	OWS	LC	NL
Palawan Reed Snake	*Calamaria palavanensis*				*			E	OWS	DD	NL
Sulu Reed Snake	*Calamaria suluensis*					*		N	OWS	LC	NL
Boie's Reed Snake	*Calamaria virgulata*				*	*		N	OWS	LC	NL
Paradise Tree Snake	*Chrysopelea paradisi paradisi*					*		N	OWS	LC	NL

English Name	Scientific Name	Luzon	West Visayas	Mindanao	Palawan	Sulu	Sub-faunal Region**	DISTRIBUTIONAL STATUS	PH RED LIST DAO 2019-09	IUCN RED LIST 2022-2	CITES
Philippine Paradise Tree Snake	Chrysopelea paradisi variabilis	*	*	*	*	*	*	E	OWS	LC	NL
Philippine Red-tailed Ratsnake	Coelognathus erythrurus erythrurus			*		*	*	N	OTS	LC	NL
Luzon Red-tailed Ratsnake	Coelognathus erythrurus manillensis	*					*	E	OTS	LC	NL
Philippine Grey-tailed Ratsnake	Coelognathus erythrurus psephenourus		*				*	E	OTS	LC	NL
Western Philippine Ratsnake	Coelognathus philippinus				*	*		E	OWS	NE	NL
Striped Bronzeback Snake	Dendrelaphis caudolineatus						*	N	OWS	LC	NL
Sulu Bronzeback Snake	Dendrelaphis flavescens					*		E	OWS	LC	NL
Negros Bronzeback Snake	Dendrelaphis fuliginosus		*				*	E	OWS	LC	NL
Leviton's Bronzeback Snake	Dendrelaphis levitoni			*				E	OWS	LC	NL
Luzon Bronzeback Snake	Dendrelaphis luzonensis	*					*	E	OWS	LC	NL
Maren's Bronzeback Snake	Dendrelaphis marenae	*	*	*	*	*	*	N	OWS	LC	NL
Philippine Bronzeback Snake	Dendrelaphis philippinensis		*	*			*	E	OWS	LC	NL
Philippine Whip Snake	Dryophiops philippina	*	*	*			*	E	OWS	DD	NL
Red Whip Snake	Dryophiops rubescens				*			N	OWS	LC	NL
Red-tailed Green Ratsnake	Gonyosoma oxycephalum	*	*	*	*	*	*	N	OTS	LC	NL
Philippine Liopeltine Snake	Liopeltis philippinus				*			E	OWS	LC	NL
Three-coloured Liopeltine Snake	Liopeltis tricolor				*	*		N	OWS	LC	NL
Alcala's Wolf Snake	Lycodon alcalai						*	E	OWS	LC	NL
Babuyan Wolf Snake	Lycodon bibonius						*	E	OWS	DD	NL
Common Wolf Snake	Lycodon capucinus	*	*	*	*		*	I	OWS	LC	NL
Dalupiri Island Wolf Snake	Lycodon chrysoprateros						*	E	OWS	CR	NL
Dumeril's Wolf Snake	Lycodon dumerilii			*			*	E	OWS	LC	NL
Faust's Wolf Snake	Lycodon fausti		*					E	OWS	LC	NL
Ferron's Wolf Snake	Lycodon ferroni						*	E	OWS	VU	NL
Müller's Wolf Snake	Lycodon muelleri	*					*	E	OWS	LC	NL
Palawan Wolf Snake	Lycodon philippinus				*			E	OWS	DD	NL
Seale's Wolf Snake	Lycodon sealei				*			E	OWS	NE	NL
Cagayan Wolf Snake	Lycodon solivagus	*						E	OWS	DD	NL
Northern Philippine Short-headed Snake	Oligodon ancorus	*					*	E	OWS	LC	NL
Spotted Short-headed Snake	Oligodon maculatus			*				E	OWS	LC	NL
Sulu Short-headed Snake	Oligodon meyerinkii					*		N	OWS	VU	NL
Spotted-bellied Short-headed Snake	Oligodon modestus		*				*	E	OWS	NT	NL
Palawan Short-headed Snake	Oligodon notospilus				*			E	OWS	LC	NL
Perkin's Short-headed Snake	Oligodon perkinsi				*			E	OWS	DD	NL
Alcala's Mountain Keelback Snake	Opisthotropis alcalai						*	E	OWS	EN	NL
Olive Mountain Keelback Snake	Opisthotropis typica			*				N	OWS	LC	NL
Zamboanga Burrowing snake	Pseudorabdion ater						*	E	OWS	DD	NL
McNamara's Burrowing Snake	Pseudorabdion mcnamarae	*	*				*	E	OWS	LC	NL
Mountain Burrowing Snake	Pseudorabdion montanum		*					E	OWS	DD	NL
Visayan Burrowing Snake	Pseudorabdion oxycephalum	*	*	*				E	OWS	LC	NL
Panay Burrowing Snake	Pseudorabdion talonuran		*					E	OWS	VU	NL
Taylor's Burrowing Snake	Pseudorabdion taylori			*				E	OWS	NT	NL
Keeled Ratsnake	Ptyas carinata				*			N	OTS	LC	NL
Philippine Smooth-scaled Mountain Ratsnake	Ptyas luzonensis	*	*				*	E	OTS	LC	NL

English Name	Scientific Name	Luzon	West Visayas	Mindanao	Palawan	Sulu	Sub-faunal Region**	DISTRIBUTIONAL STATUS	PH RED LIST DAO 2019-09	IUCN RED LIST 2022-2	CITES
White-lined Keelback Snake	*Rhabdophis auriculatus auriculatus*			*			*	E	OWS	LC	NL
Myers' Keelback Snake	*Rhabdophis auriculatus myersi*			*			*	E	OWS	LC	NL
Barbour's Keelback Snake	*Rhabdophis barbouri*	*						E	OWS	DD	NL
Spekle-bellied Keelback Snake	*Rhabdophis chrysargos*				*			N	OWS	LC	NL
Striped Keelback Snake	*Rhabdophis lineatus*			*			*	E	OWS	LC	NL
Palawan Yellow-striped Snake	*Sibynophis bivittatus*				*			E	OWS	LC	NL
Black-headed Many-toothed Snake	*Sibynophis geminatus geminatus*					*		N	OWS	LC	NL
Philippine Cave Snake	*Stegonotus muelleri*			*			*	E	OWS	LC	NL
Mindanao Spotted Water Snake	*Tropidonophis dendrophiops*			*			*	E	OWS	LC	NL
Negros Spotted Water Snake	*Tropidonophis negrosensis*		*				*	E	OWS	NT	NL
Luzon Keelback Snake	*Tropidonophis spilogaster*	*					*	E	OWS	LC	NL
Cyclocoridae (Cyclocorids)											
Alcala's Triangle-spotted Snake	*Cyclocorus lineatus alcalai*		*				*	E	OWS	LC	NL
Luzon Triangle-spotted Snake	*Cyclocorus lineatus lineatus*	*					*	E	OWS	LC	NL
Southern Triangle-spotted Snake	*Cyclocorus nuchalis nuchalis*			*				E	OWS	LC	NL
Taylor's Triangle-spotted Snake	*Cyclocorus nuchalis taylori*			*			*	E	OWS	LC	NL
Panay White-lipped Snake	*Hologerrhum dermali*		*				*	E	OWS	EN	NL
Luzon White-lipped Snake	*Hologerrhum philippinum*	*					*	E	OWS	LC	NL
Waray Drawf Burrowing Snake	*Levitonius mirus*						*	E	OWS	DD	NL
Mountain Province Snake	*Myersophis alpestris*	*						E	OWS	DD	NL
Luzon Shrub Snake	*Oxyrhabdium leporinum leporinum*	*					*	E	OWS	LC	NL
Visayan Shrub Snake	*Oxyrhabdium leporinum visayanum*		*					E	OWS	LC	NL
Mindanao Shrub Snake	*Oxyrhabdium modestum*			*			*	E	OWS	LC	NL
Elapidae (Elapids)											
Two-lined Coral Snake	*Calliophis bilineatus*				*			E	OWS	NE	NL
Malayan Blue Coral Snake	*Calliophis bivirgatus flaviceps*				*			I	OWS	LC	NL
Philippine Coral Snake	*Calliophis philippinus*			*			*	E	OWS	NE	NL
Dinagat Banded Coral Snake	*Calliophis salitan*			*				E	OWS	DD	NL
Sulu Coral Snake	*Calliophis suluensis*					*		E	OWS	NE	NL
Luzon Barred Coral Snake	*Hemibungarus calligaster*	*					*	E	OWS	LC	NL
Central Philippine Barred Coral Snake	*Hemibungarus gemianulis*		*					E	OWS	LC	NL
McClung's Barred Coral Snake	*Hemibungarus mcclungi*	*					*	E	OWS	LC	NL
Northern Philippine Cobra	*Naja philippinensis*	*	*				*	E	OTS	NT	II
Southern Philippine Cobra	*Naja samarensis*		*	*			*	E	OTS	LC	II
Palawan Spitting Cobra	*Naja sumatrana miolepis*				*			N	OTS	LC	II
King Cobra	*Ophiophagus hannah*	*	*	*	*	*	*	N	OTS	VU	II
Turtle-headed Sea Snake	*Emydocephalus annulatus*		*	*				N	OWS	LC	NL
Black-headed Sea Snake	*Hydrophis atriceps*	*	*	*		*		N	OWS	LC	NL
Belcher's Sea Snake	*Hydrophis belcheri*		*					N	OWS	DD	NL
Short Sea Snake	*Hydrophis curtus*	*	*	*				N	OWS	LC	NL
Annulated Sea Snake	*Hydrophis cyanocinctus*		*	*				N	OWS	LC	NL
Lambert's Sea Snake	*Hydrophis lamberti*	*	*					N	OWS	LC	NL
Black-headed Sea Snake	*Hydrophis melanocephalus*							N	OWS	DD	NL
Ornate Reef Sea Snake	*Hydrophis ornatus*	*	*					N	OWS	LC	NL
Yellow-bellied Sea Snake	*Hydrophis platurus*	*	*	*		*		N	OWS	LC	NL

English Name	Scientific Name	Luzon	West Visayas	Mindanao	Palawan	Sulu	Sub-faunal Region**	DISTRIBUTIONAL STATUS	PH RED LIST DAO 2019-09	IUCN RED LIST 2022-2	CITES
Lake Taal Sea Snake	*Hydrophis semperi*	*						E	OWS	VU	NL
Yellow Sea Snake	*Hydrophis spiralis*							N	OWS	LC	NL
Stoke's Sea Snake	*Hydrophis stokesii*			*				N	OWS	LC	NL
Graceful Small-headed Sea Snake	*Microcephalophis gracilis*	*						N	OWS	LC	NL
Yellow-lipped Sea Krait	*Laticauda colubrina*	*	*	*		*	*	N	OWS	LC	NL
Blue-lipped Sea Krait	*Laticauda laticaudata*	*	*	*			*	N	OWS	LC	NL
Half-banded Sea Krait	*Laticauda semifasciata*	*	*	*	*	*		N	OWS	NT	NL
Gerrhopilidae (Blind Snakes)											
Negros Island Worm Snake	*Gerrhopilus hedraeus*	*	*	*			*	E	OWS	LC	NL
Manila Worm Snake	*Gerrhopilus manilae*	*						E	OWS	DD	NL
Homalopsidae (Water Snakes)											
Lake Buhi Dog-faced Water Snake	*Cerberus microlepis*						*	E	OWS	DD	NL
Schneider's Dog-faced Water Snake	*Cerberus schneiderii*	*	*	*	*	*	*	N	OWS	NE	NL
Crab-eating Snake	*Fordonia leucobalia*			*				N	OWS	LC	NL
Cat-eyed Water Snake	*Gerarda prevostiana*				*			N	OWS	LC	NL
Pareidae (Snail-eating Snakes)											
Blunthead Slug Snake	*Aplopeltura boa*		*	*	*	*		N	OWS	LC	NL
Pseudaspididae (Mock Snakes, Keeled Snakes & Mock Vipers)											
Common Mock Viper	*Psammodynastes pulverulentus pulverulentus*	*	*	*	*	*	*	N	OWS	LC	NL
Pythonidae (Pythons)											
Reticulated Python	*Malayopython reticulatus reticulatus*	*	*	*	*	*	*	N	OTS	LC	II
Typhlopidae (Worm Snakes)											
Banao Worm Snake	*Acutotyphlops banaorum*	*						E	OWS	DD	NL
Brahminy Worm Snake	*Indotyphlops braminus*	*	*	*	*	*	*	I	OWS	LC	NL
Andy's Worm Snake	*Malayotyphlops andyi*	*						E	OWS	DD	NL
Canlaon Worm Snake	*Malayotyphlops canlaonensis*		*					E	OWS	DD	NL
Brown-backed Worm Snake	*Malayotyphlops castanotus*		*					E	OWS	LC	NL
Collared Worm Snake	*Malayotyphlops collaris*						*	E	OWS	DD	NL
DENR Worm Snake	*Malayotyphlops denrorum*	*						E	OWS	DD	NL
Cebu Worm Snake	*Malayotyphlops hypogius*		*					E	OWS	DD	NL
Luzon Worm Snake	*Malayotyphlops luzonensis*	*	*				*	E	OWS	LC	NL
Red Worm Snake	*Malayotyphlops ruber*						*	E	OWS	LC	NL
Red-tailed Worm Snake	*Malayotyphlops ruficauda*	*	*				*	E	OWS	DD	NL
Cuming's Worm Snake	*Ramphotyphlops cumingii*	*	*	*			*	E	OWS	DD	NL
Marx's Worm Snake	*Ramphotyphlops marxi*						*	E	OWS	DD	NL
Olive Worm Snake	*Ramphotyphlops olivaceus*			*		*	*	N	OWS	LC	NL
Sulu Worm Snake	*Ramphotyphlops suluensis*					*	*	E	OWS	VU	NL
Viperidae (Vipers)											
Philippine Yellow-spotted Pitviper	*Trimeresurus flavomaculatus*	*	*	*			*	E	OTS	LC	NL
McGregor's Pitviper	*Trimeresurus mcgregori*						*	E	EN	EN	NL
Schultze's Pitviper	*Trimeresurus schultzei*				*			E	OTS	LC	NL
Southern Philippine Keel-throated Pitviper	*Tropidolaemus philippensis*			*				E	OTS	LC	NL
Banded Keel-throated Pitviper	*Tropidolaemus subannulatus*	*	*	*	*	*	*	N	OTS	LC	NL

English Name	Scientific Name	Luzon	West Visayas	Mindanao	Palawan	Sulu	Sub-faunal Region**	DISTRIBUTIONAL STATUS	PH RED LIST DAO 2019-09	IUCN RED LIST 2022-2	CITES
Xenopeltidae (Sunbeam Snakes)											
Sunbeam Snake	Xenopeltis unicolor				*	*		N	OWS	LC	NL
Cheloniidae (Sea Turtles)											
Loggerhead Sea Turtle	Caretta caretta		*	*	*			N	EN	VU	I
Pacific Hawksbill Sea Turtle	Eretmochelys imbricata bissa	*	*	*	*		*	N	CR	CR	I
Olive Ridley Sea Turtle	Lepidochelys olivacea	*	*	*	*			N	EN	VU	I
Green Sea Turtle	Chelonia mydas	*	*	*	*	*	*	N	EN	EN	I
Dermochelyidae (Leatherback Sea Turtle)											
Leatherback Sea Turtle	Dermochelys coriacea	*	*		*		*	N	CR	VU	I
Emydidae (New World Pond Turtles)											
Painted Turtle	Chrysemys picta	*						I	OWS	LC	NL
Red-eared slider	Trachemys scripta elegans	*	*	*				I	OWS	LC	NL
Geoemydidae (Old World Pond Turtles)											
Philippine Box Turtle	Cuora philippinensis	*	*	*			*	E	OTS	NE	II
Sunda Box Turtle	Cuora cf. couro				*	*		N	OTS	EN	II
Asian Leaf Turtle	Cyclemys dentata				*	*		N	VU	NT	II
Spiny Turtle	Heosemys spinosa				*			N	EN	EN	II
Philippine Forest Turtle	Siebenrockiella leytensis				*			E	CR	CR	II
Trionychidae (Softshell Turtles)											
Malayan Softshell Turtle	Dogania subplana				*			N	OWS	LC	II
Asian Giant Softshell Turtle	Pelochelys cantorii	*		*				N	OTS	CR	II
Chinese Softshell Turtle	Pelodiscus sinensis	*	*	*			*	I	OWS	VU	NL

** Occurs in one or more subfaunal regions

~ Appendix II for Saltwater Crocodile populations of Australia, Indonesia, Malaysia, Papua New Guinea, and Palawan (Philippines).

Sy, E. Y. (ed). 2023. Checklist of the reptiles of the Philippines, version 2023-2. Reptile & Amphibian Database Philippines. www.herpetologyph.com

FURTHER READING

Diesmos, A. C., Brown, R. M., Alcala, A. C. & Sison, R.V. 2008. Status and distribution of nonmarine turtles of the Philippines. *Chelonian Conservation and Biology* 7(2): 157–177.

Diesmos, A. C., Buskirk, J. R., Schoppe, S., Diesmos, M. L. L., Sy, E. Y. & Brown, R. M. 2012. *Siebenrockiella leytensis* (Taylor 1920) – Palawan Forest Turtle, Philippine Forest Turtle. In: Rhodin, A. G. J., Pritchard, P. P., van Dijk, R. A., Saumure, K.A., Buhlmann, J. B. Iverson & Mittermeier R. A. (eds.). Conservation Biology of Freshwater Turtles and Tortoises: A Compilation Project of the IUCN/SSC Tortoise and Freshwater Turtle Specialist Group. *Chelonian Research Monographs* 5: 066.1–066.9.

Gaulke, M. 2011. *The Herpetofauna of Panay Island, Philippines: An Illustrated Field Guide*. Edition Chimaira, Frankfurt am Maim, Germany.

Leviton, A. E., Siler, C. D., Weinell, J. L. & Brown, R. M. 2018. Synopsis of the snakes of the Philippines. *Proceedings of the California Academy of Sciences*, series 4, 64(14): 399–568.

Linkem, C. W., Diesmos, A. C. & Brown, R. M. 2011. Molecular systematics of the Philippine forest skinks (Squamata: Scincidae: *Sphenomorphus*): testing morphological hypotheses of interspecific relationships. *Zoological Journal of the Linnean Society* 163: 1217–1243.

Siler, C. D., Diesmos, A. C., Alcala, A. C. & Brown, R. M. 2011. Phylogeny of Philippine slender skinks (Scincidae: *Brachymeles*) reveals underestimated species diversity, complex biogeographical relationships, and cryptic patterns of lineage diversification. *Molecular Phylogenetics and Evolution* 59: 53–65.

Siler, C. D., Oaks, J. R., Esselstyn, J. A., Diesmos, A. C. & Brown, R. M. 2010. Phylogeny and biogeography of Philippine bent-toed geckos (Gekkonidae: *Cyrtodactylus*) contradicts a prevailing model of Pleistocene diversification. *Molecular Phylogenetics and Evolution* 55: 699–710.

Supsup, C. E. et al. 2016. Amphibians and reptiles of Cebu, Philippines: the poorly understood herpetofauna of an island with very little remaining natural habitat. *Asian Herpetological Research* 7(3): 151–179.

Sy, E. Y. (2018). Trading Faces: utilisation of Facebook to trade live reptiles in the Philippines. TRAFFIC, Petaling Jaya, Selangor, Malaysia. vii.

Sy, E. Y. (ed). 2023. Checklist of reptiles of the Philippines, version 2023–4. Reptile & Amphibian Database Philippines. www.herpetologyph.com

Sy, E. Y., Schoppe, S., Diesmos, M. L. L., Lim, T. M. S. & Diesmos, A.C. 2020. Endangered by trade: seizure analysis of the critically endangered Philippine Forest Turtle *Siebenrockiella leytensis* from 2004–2018. *Philippine Journal of Systematic Biology* 14(2). DOI: 10.26757/pjsb2020b14003

van Weerd, M. & van der Ploeg, J. 2012. *The Philippine Crocodile: Ecology, Culture and Conservation.* Mabuwaya Foundation, Cabagan, Isabela, Philippines.

Weinell, J. L., Hooper, E., Leviton, A. E. & Brown, R. M. 2019. Illustrated key to the snakes of the Philippines. *Proceedings of the California Academy of Sciences* series 4, 66: 1–49.

Welton, L. J., Siler, C. D., Grismer, L. L., Diesmos, A. C., Sites, J. W. & Brown, R. M. 2017). Archipelago-wide survey of Philippine forest dragons (Agamidae: *Gonocephalus*): multilocus phylogeny uncovers unprecedented levels of genetic diversity in a biodiversity hotspot. *Biological Journal of the Linnean Society* 120: 410–426.

ACKNOWLEDGEMENTS

This field guide is the author's modest attempt to provide a brief introduction to the diverse and amazing reptiles of the Philippines to budding herpetologists, visiting naturalists, and anyone interested in identifying the animals they see in the wild. Several species are illustrated in colour for the first time, and this was made possible by the generous contributions of photographs from friends and colleagues. My heartfelt gratitude also goes out to John Beaufoy, Rosemary Wilkinson, Krystyna Mayer and the production team for their guidance and unwavering support.